Cambridge Latin Course

Cambridge Latin Course

Book IV

FOURTH EDITION

CAMBRIDGE
UNIVERSITY PRESS

CAMBRIDGE UNIVERSITY PRESS
Cambridge, New York, Melbourne, Madrid, Cape Town, Singapore, São Paulo

Cambridge University Press
The Edinburgh Building, Cambridge CB2 8RU, UK

www.cambridge.org
Information on this title: www.cambridge.org/9780521797931

This book, an outcome of work jointly commissioned by the Schools Council before its closure and the Cambridge School Classics Project, is published under the aegis of Qualifications and Curriculum Authority Enterprises Limited, 83 Piccadilly, London W1J 8QA.

First published 1971
7th printing 1982
Second edition 1984
5th printing 1988
Integrated edition 1990
11th printing 2000
Fourth edition 2002
7th printing 2007

Printed in the United Kingdom at the University Press, Cambridge

A catalogue record for this publication is available from the British Library

ISBN 978-0-521-79793-1 paperback

Cover photographs: front, head of Haterius, Photo Scala, Florence; model of Rome, Museo della Civiltà Romana; back, Photo Scala, Florence.
Drawings by Peter Kesteven, Joy Mellor, Leslie Jones and Roger Dalladay

ACKNOWLEDGEMENTS

Thanks are due to the following for supplying photographs and drawings for reproduction: p. 6, Nathan Meron; p. 17, Alberto Carpececi *Rome 2000 Years Ago* pub. Bonechi; p. 19 *t, b*, p. 20 *b*, Margaret Widdess; p. 21, Baron Wolman; p. 22, Fitzwilliam Museum, Cambridge; p. 23, p. 31 *l, r*, p. 35 *l*, p. 52 *b*, Photo Scala, Florence; p. 35 *r*, J. P. Adam *Roman Building* pub. Batsford; p. 36, © St Albans Museums; p. 52, p. 72, Cambridge School Classics Project; p. 59, Manchester Museum; p. 76, Courtesy of the Museum of London; p. 81 *b*, p. 90 *b*, p. 91 *b*, p. 92, p. 111, © Copyright The British Museum; p. 89, Visual Publications; p.91, Kunsthistorisches Museum, Vienna; p. 93, p. 106, Musée royal du Mariemont, Morlanwelz, Belgium; p. 101, German Archaeological Institute, Rome.

Other photography by Roger Dalladay. Thanks are due to the following for permission to reproduce photographs: p. 1, p. 65, Museo della Civiltà Romana; p. 10, p. 15, p. 18 c, p. 18 *b*, p. 71, Roman Forum; p. 51 *b*, Vatican Museums; p. 56, p. 77, Museo Archeologico Nazionale, Naples; p. 73, Antiquario, Castellammare di Stabia; p. 38, p. 74, p. 105, The British Museum; p. 90, Chieti Museum; p. 93, p. 95, Museo Nazionale Romano; p. 107 *t, b*, Soprintendenza, Pompeii.

Every effort has been made to reach copyright holders. The publishers would be glad to hear from anyone whose rights they have unknowingly infringed.

Contents

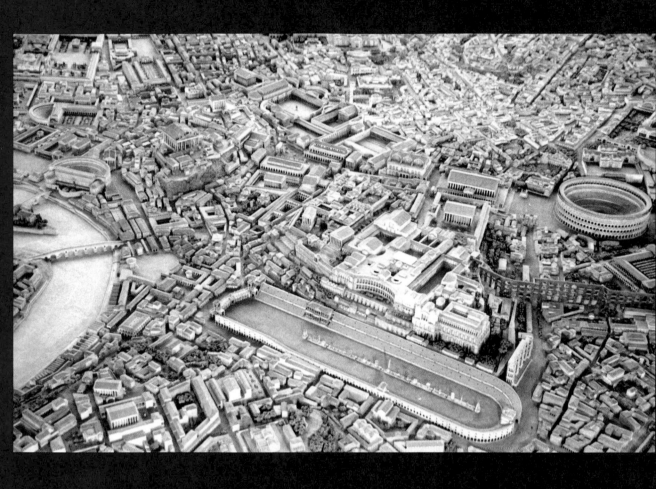

ROMA

STAGE 29

1   in mediā Rōmā est mōns nōtissimus, quī Capitōlium
    appellātur.
    in summō Capitōliō stat templum, ubi deus Iuppiter adōrātur.

2   sub Capitōliō iacet Forum Rōmānum.
    forum ab ingentī multitūdine cīvium cotīdiē complētur.
    aliī negōtium agunt; aliī in porticibus stant et ab amīcīs
    salūtantur; aliī per forum in lectīcīs feruntur. ubīque magnus
    strepitus audītur.

3 aliquandō pompae splendidae per forum dūcuntur.

4 prope medium forum est templum Vestae, ubi ignis sacer ā Virginibus Vestālibus cūrātur.

5 in extrēmō forō stant Rōstra, ubi ōrātiōnēs apud populum habentur.

6 prope Rōstra est carcer, ubi captīvī populī Rōmānī custōdiuntur.

nox

I

nox erat. lūna stēllaeque in caelō serēnō fulgēbant. tempus erat
quō hominēs quiēscere solent. Rōmae tamen nūlla erat quiēs,
nūllum silentium.

    magnīs in domibus, ubi dīvitēs habitābant, cēnae splendidae
cōnsūmēbantur. cibus sūmptuōsus ā servīs offerēbātur; vīnum   *5*
optimum ab ancillīs fundēbātur; carmina ā citharoedīs
perītissimīs cantābantur.

    in altīs autem īnsulīs, nūllae cēnae splendidae
cōnsūmēbantur, nūllī citharoedī audiēbantur. ibi pauperēs, famē
paene cōnfectī, vītam miserrimam agēbant. aliī ad patrōnōs   *10*
epistulās scrībēbant ut auxilium eōrum peterent, aliī scelera
committere parābant.

    prope forum magnus strepitus audiēbātur. nam arcus
magnificus in Viā Sacrā exstruēbātur. ingēns polyspaston arcuī
imminēbat. fabrī, quī arcum exstruēbant, dīligentissimē   *15*
labōrābant. aliī figūrās in arcū sculpēbant; aliī titulum in
fronte arcūs īnscrībēbant; aliī marmor ad summum arcum
tollēbant. omnēs strēnuē labōrābant ut arcum ante lūcem
perficerent. nam Imperātor Domitiānus hunc arcum frātrī Titō
postrīdiē dēdicāre volēbat. Titum vīvum ōderat; sed Titum   *20*
mortuum honōrāre cupiēbat. Domitiānus enim populum
Rōmānum, quī Titum maximē dīlēxerat, nunc sibi favēre
volēbat.

II

praeerat huic operī Quīntus Haterius Latrōniānus, redēmptor
nōtissimus. eā nocte ipse fabrōs furēns incitābat. aderat quoque
Gāius Salvius Līberālis, Haterii patrōnus, quī eum invicem
incitābat ut opus ante lūcem perficeret. anxius enim erat Salvius
quod Imperātōrī persuāserat ut Haterium operī praeficeret. hic   *5*
igitur fabrīs, quamquam omnīnō fessī erant, identidem
imperāvit nē labōre dēsisterent.

    Glitus, magister fabrōrum, Haterium lēnīre temptābat.

    'ecce, domine!' inquit. 'fabrī iam arcum paene perfēcērunt.
ultimae litterae titulī nunc īnscrībuntur; ultimae figūrae   *10*
sculpuntur; ultimae marmoris massae ad summum arcum
tolluntur.'

serēnō: serēnus *calm, clear*
fulgēbant: fulgēre *shine*
tempus *time*
Rōmae *at Rome*
quiēs *rest*
domibus: domus *house, home*
carmina: carmen *song*
altīs: altus *high*
īnsulīs: īnsula *block of flats*
famē: famēs *hunger*
cōnfectī: cōnfectus *worn out,
   exhausted*
patrōnōs: patrōnus *patron*
arcus *arch*
Viā Sacrā: Via Sacra *the Sacred
   Way (road running through
   the Forum)*
polyspaston *crane*
fabrī: faber *craftsman,
   workman*
figūrās: figūra *figure, shape*
sculpēbant: sculpere *carve*
titulum: titulus *inscription*
fronte: frōns *front*
īnscrībēbant: īnscrībere *write,
   inscribe*
marmor *marble*
ante *before*
lūcem: lūx *light, daylight*
perficerent: perficere *finish*
dēdicāre *dedicate*

operī: opus *work, construction*
redēmptor *contractor, builder*
invicem *in turn*

identidem *repeatedly*

lēnīre *soothe, calm down*

ultimae: ultimus *last*
litterae: littera *letter*
massae: massa *block*

paulō ante hōram prīmam, fabrī labōre cōnfectī arcum perfēcērunt. paulīsper urbs silēbat.

ūnus faber tamen, domum per forum rediēns, subitō trīstēs 15
fēminārum duārum clāmōrēs audīvit. duae enim captīvae,
magnō dolōre affectae, in carcere cantābant:

'mī Deus! mī Deus! respice mē! quārē mē dēseruistī?'

15

paulīsper *for a short time*
silēbat: silēre *be silent*
dolōre: dolor *grief*
affectae: affectus *affected, overcome*
respice: respicere *look at, look upon*
quārē? *why?*

'ecce domine! fabrī iam arcum paene perfēcērunt.'

Masada

I

ex carcere, ubi captīvī custōdiēbantur, trīstēs clāmōrēs
audiēbantur. duae enim fēminae Iūdaeae, superstitēs eōrum quī
contrā Rōmānōs rebellāverant, fortūnam suam lūgēbant. altera
erat anus septuāgintā annōrum, altera mātrōna trīgintā annōs
nāta. ūnā cum eīs in carcere erant quīnque līberī, quōrum Simōn   5
nātū maximus sōlācium mātrī et aviae ferre temptābat.

    'māter, nōlī lūgēre! decōrum est Iūdaeīs fortitūdinem in rēbus
adversīs praestāre.'

    māter fīlium amplexa,

    'melius erat', inquit, 'cum patre vestrō perīre abhinc annōs   10
novem. cūr tum ā morte abhorruī? cūr vōs servāvī?'

    Simōn, hīs verbīs commōtus, mātrem rogāvit quō modō
periisset pater atque quārē rem prius nōn nārrāvisset. eam ōrāvit
ut omnia explicāret. sed tantus erat dolor mātris ut prīmō nihil
dīcere posset. mox, cum sē collēgisset, ad fīliōs conversa,   15

    'dē morte patris vestrī', inquit, 'prius nārrāre nōlēbam nē vōs
quoque perīrētis, exemplum eius imitātī. nunc tamen audeō
vōbīs tōtam rem patefacere quod nōs omnēs crās moritūrī
sumus.

Iūdaeae: Iūdaeus *Jewish*
superstitēs: superstes
  survivor
rebellāverant: rebellāre *rebel,*
  revolt
lūgēbant: lūgēre *lament,*
  mourn, grieve
altera ... altera *one ... the other*
... annōs nāta *... years old*
ūnā cum *together with*
nātū maximus *eldest*
aviae: avia *grandmother*
rēbus adversīs: rēs adversae
  misfortune
praestāre *show, display*
amplexa: amplexus *having*
  embraced
abhinc *ago*
abhorruī: abhorrēre *shrink*
  (from)
exemplum *example*
imitātī: imitātus *having*
  imitated
crās *tomorrow*

The rock of Masada, showing the Roman siege ramp built on the west (left) side.

nōs Iūdaeī contrā Rōmānōs trēs annōs rebellāvimus. annō
quārtō iste Beelzebub, Titus, urbem Ierosolymam expugnāvit.
numquam ego spectāculum terribilius vīdī: ubīque aedificia
flammīs cōnsūmēbantur; ubīque virī, fēminae, līberī
occīdēbantur; Templum ipsum ā mīlitibus dīripiēbātur; tōta
urbs ēvertēbātur. in illā clāde periērunt multa mīlia Iūdaeōrum;
sed circiter mīlle superstitēs, duce Eleazārō, rūpem Masadam
occupāvērunt. tū, Simōn, illō tempore vix quīnque annōs nātus
erās.
   'rūpēs Masada est alta et praerupta, prope lacum Asphaltītēn
sita. ibi nōs, mūnītiōnibus undique dēfēnsī, Rōmānīs diū
resistēbāmus. intereā dux hostium, Lūcius Flāvius Silva, rūpem
castellīs multīs circumvēnit. deinde mīlitēs, iussū Silvae,
ingentem aggerem usque ad summam rūpem exstrūxērunt.
postrēmō aggerem ascendērunt, magnamque partem
mūnītiōnum ignī dēlēvērunt. tandem, cum nox appropinquāret,
Silva mīlitēs ad castra redūxit ut proximum diem victōriamque
exspectārent.'

<table>
<tr><td>20</td><td></td></tr>
<tr><td>25</td><td></td></tr>
<tr><td>30</td><td></td></tr>
<tr><td>35</td><td></td></tr>
</table>

Beelzebub *Beelzebub, devil*
Ierosolymam: Ierosolyma
   Jerusalem
expugnāvit: expugnāre *storm,*
   take by storm
circiter *about*
duce: dux *leader*
rūpem: rūpēs *rock, crag*
praerupta: praeruptus *sheer,*
   steep
lacum Asphaltītēn: lacus
   Asphaltītēs *Lake Asphaltites*
   (the Dead Sea)
mūnītiōnibus: mūnītiō
   defence, fortification
undique *on all sides*
castellīs: castellum *fort*
iussū Silvae *at Silva's order*
aggerem: agger *ramp, mound*
usque ad *right up to*
ignī, *abl*: ignis *fire*

II

'illā nocte Eleazārus Iūdaeīs cōnsilium dīrum prōposuit.
   '"magnō in discrīmine sumus", inquit. "nōs Iūdaeī, Deō
cōnfīsī, Rōmānīs adhūc resistimus; nunc illī nōs in servitūtem
trahere parant. nūlla spēs salūtis nōbīs ostenditur. nōnne melius
est perīre quam Rōmānīs cēdere? ego ipse mortem meā manū
īnflīctam accipiō, servitūtem spernō."
   'hīs verbīs Eleazārus tantum ardōrem in Iūdaeīs excitāvit ut
ad mortem statim festīnārent. virī uxōrēs līberōsque amplexī
occīdērunt. cum hanc dīram et saevam rem cōnfēcissent, decem
eōrum sorte ductī cēterōs interfēcērunt. tum ūnus ex illīs, sorte
invicem ductus, postquam novem reliquōs interfēcit, sē ipsum
gladiō trānsfīxit.'
   'quō modō nōs ipsī effūgimus?' rogāvit Simōn.
   'ego Eleazārō pārēre nōn potuī', respondit māter. 'vōbīscum
in locō subterrāneō latēbam.'
   'ignāva!' clāmāvit Simōn. 'ego mortem haudquāquam timeō.
ego, patris exemplī memor, eandem fortitūdinem praestāre
volō.'

<table>
<tr><td>5</td><td></td></tr>
<tr><td>10</td><td></td></tr>
<tr><td>15</td><td></td></tr>
</table>

discrīmine: discrīmen *crisis*
cōnfīsī: cōnfīsus *having*
   trusted, having put trust
servitūtem: servitūs *slavery*
īnflīctam: īnflīgere *inflict*
ardōrem: ardor *spirit,*
   enthusiasm

sorte ductī *chosen by lot*
reliquōs: reliquus *remaining*
trānsfīxit: trānsfīgere *stab*

subterrāneō: subterrāneus
   underground
haudquāquam *not at all*
memor *remembering, mindful of*
eandem *the same*

About the language 1: passive verbs

1 In Book I, you met sentences like these:

> puer clāmōrem **audit**.   ancilla vīnum **fundēbat**.
> *A boy **hears** the shout.*   *A slave-girl **was pouring** wine.*

The words in **bold type** are active forms of the verb.

2 In Stage 29, you have met sentences like these:

> clāmor ā puerō **audītur**.   vīnum ab ancillā **fundēbātur**.
> *The shout **is heard** by a boy.*   *Wine **was being poured** by a slave-girl.*

The words in **bold type** are passive forms of the verb.

3 Compare the following active and passive forms:

present tense

present active	*present passive*
portat	portātur
s/he carries, s/he is carrying	*s/he is carried*, or *s/he is being carried*

portant	portantur
they carry, they are carrying	*they are carried*, or *they are being carried*

imperfect tense

imperfect active	*imperfect passive*
portābat	portābātur
s/he was carrying	*s/he was being carried*

portābant	portābantur
they were carrying	*they were being carried*

4 Further examples of the present passive:

a cēna nostra ā coquō nunc parātur.
b multa scelera in hāc urbe cotīdiē committuntur.
c laudantur; dūcitur; rogātur; mittuntur.

Further examples of the imperfect passive:

d candidātī ab amīcīs salūtābantur.
e fābula ab āctōribus in theātrō agēbātur.
f audiēbantur; laudābātur; necābantur; tenēbātur.

arcus Titī

I

postrīdiē māne ingēns Rōmānōrum multitūdō ad arcum Titī
undique conveniēbat. diēs fēstus ab omnibus cīvibus
celebrābātur. Imperātor Domitiānus eō diē frātrī Titō arcum
dēdicātūrus erat. iussū Imperātōris pompa magnifica tōtam per
urbem dūcēbātur.   5

    multae sellae ā servīs prope arcum pōnēbantur. illūc multī
senātōrēs, spē favōris Domitiānī, conveniēbant. inter eōs Salvius,
togam splendidam gerēns, locum quaerēbat ubi cōnspicuus
esset. inter equitēs, quī post senātōrēs stābant, aderat Haterius
ipse. favōrem Imperātōris avidē spērābat, et in animō volvēbat   10
quandō ā Salviō praemium prōmissum acceptūrus esset.

    āra ingēns, prō arcū exstrūcta, ā servīs flōribus ōrnābātur.
circum āram stābant vīgintī sacerdōtēs. aderant quoque
haruspicēs quī exta victimārum īnspicerent.

    intereā pompa lentē per Viam Sacram dūcēbātur. prīmā in   15
parte incēdēbant tubicinēs, tubās īnflantēs. post eōs vēnērunt
iuvenēs, quī trīgintā taurōs corōnīs ōrnātōs ad sacrificium
dūcēbant. tum multī servī, quī gāzam Iūdaeōrum portābant,
prīmam pompae partem claudēbant. huius gāzae pars
pretiōsissima erat mēnsa sacra, tubae, candēlābrum, quae omnia 20
aurea erant.

    septem captīvī Iūdaeī, quī mediā in pompā incēdēbant, ā
spectātōribus vehementer dērīdēbantur. quīnque puerī, serēnō
vultū incēdentēs, clāmōrēs et contumēliās neglegēbant, sed duae
fēminae plūrimīs lacrimīs spectātōrēs ōrābant ut līberīs   25
parcerent.

    post captīvōs vēnit Domitiānus ipse, currū magnificō vectus.
post Imperātōrem ībant ambō cōnsulēs, quōrum alter erat L.
Flāvius Silva. magistrātūs nōbilissimī effigiem Titī in umerīs
portābant. ā mīlitibus pompa claudēbātur.   30

undique *from all sides*

dēdicātūrus *going to dedicate*

favōris: favor *favour*
cōnspicuus *conspicuous, easily
  seen*
equitēs *equites (well-to-do men
  ranking below senators)*
quandō *when*
acceptūrus *going to receive*
exta *entrails*

incēdēbant: incēdere *march,
  stride*
gāzam: gāza *treasure*
claudēbant: claudere
  conclude, complete

vultū: vultus *expression, face*

currū: currus *chariot*
vectus: vehere *carry*
cōnsulēs: cōnsul *consul (senior
  magistrate)*
magistrātūs: magistrātus
  *magistrate (elected official of
  Roman government)*

II

When you have read this part of the story, answer the questions on the next page.

ad arcum pompa pervēnit. Domitiānus, ē currū ēgressus ut sacrificium faceret, senātōrēs equitēsque salūtāvit. tum oculōs in arcum ipsum convertit. admīrātiōne affectus, Imperātor Salvium ad sē arcessītum valdē laudāvit. eī imperāvit ut Hateriō grātiās ageret. inde ad āram prōgressus, cultrum cēpit quō victimam sacrificāret. servus eī iugulum taurī obtulit. deinde Domitiānus victimam sacrificāvit, haec locūtus:

    'tibi, dīve Tite, haec victima nunc sacrificātur; tibi hic arcus dēdicātur; tibi grātiae maximae ā populō Rōmānō aguntur.'

    subitō, dum Rōmānī oculōs in sacrificium intentē dēfīgunt, Simōn occāsiōnem nactus prōsiluit. mediōs in sacerdōtēs irrūpit; cultrum rapuit. omnēs spectātōrēs immōtī stābant, audāciā eius attonitī. Domitiānus, pavōre commōtus, pedem rettulit. nōn Imperātōrem tamen Simōn petīvit. cultrum in manū tenēns clāmāvit,

    'nōs, quī superstitēs Iūdaeōrum rebellantium sumus, Rōmānīs servīre nōlumus. mortem obīre mālumus.'

    haec locūtus, facinus dīrum commīsit. mātrem et aviam amplexus cultrō statim occīdit. tum frātrēs, haudquāquam resistentēs, eōdem modō interfēcit. postrēmō magnā vōce populum Rōmānum dētestātus sē ipsum cultrō trānsfīxit.

admīrātiōne: admīrātiō *admiration*
5 **inde** *then*
cultrum: culter *knife*

dīve: dīvus *god*

10 **dum** *while*
dēfīgunt: dēfīgere *fix*
occāsiōnem: occāsiō *opportunity*
nactus *having seized*
prōsiluit: prōsilīre *leap forward, jump*
15 **pavōre: pavor** *panic*
pedem rettulit: pedem referre *step back*
servīre *serve (as a slave)*
20 **mālumus: mālle** *prefer*
eōdem modō *in the same way*
dētestātus *having cursed*

Carving on the arch of Titus, showing the treasures of the Temple at Jerusalem carried in triumph through the streets of Rome.

Questions

		Marks

1 What was Domitian's purpose when he left his chariot (lines 1–2)? — 1

2 What did he do next (line 2)? — 1

3 **admīrātiōne** (line 3). What caused this feeling? What did it prompt the emperor to do? — 1 + 2

4 What order did the emperor give to Salvius? — 1

5 Why do you think the emperor did not wish to meet Haterius personally? — 1

6 **inde ... obtulit** (lines 5–6). Describe how the victim was to be sacrificed. — 1

7 To whom were the emperor's words addressed (lines 8–9)? — 1

8 What three points did he make in his speech (lines 8–9)? — 3

9 **subitō ... prōsiluit** (lines 10–11). Why did Simon's action at first pass unnoticed? — 1

10 **mediōs in sacerdōtēs irrūpit** (line 11). Why did he do this? — 1

11 Write down the Latin phrase that explains the reaction of the spectators (lines 12–13). — 1

12 Why do you think Domitian was **pavōre commōtus** (line 13)? — 1

13 **mātrem ... interfēcit** (lines 18–20). Describe Simon's actions. — 3

14 Describe Simon's death (lines 20–1). — 2

15 Look back at lines 16–21. In what ways did Simon's words and actions copy those of Eleazarus at Masada (Masada II, lines 2–12)? — 2 + 2

TOTAL **25**

About the language 2: more about purpose clauses

1 In Stage 26, you met purpose clauses used with **ut**:

> senex īnsidiās parāvit **ut fūrēs caperet**.
> *The old man set a trap in order that he might catch the thieves.*

Or, in more natural English:
> *The old man set a trap to catch the thieves.*

2 In Stage 29, you have met purpose clauses used with the relative pronoun **quī**:

> fēmina servum mīsit **quī cibum emeret**.
> *The woman sent a slave who was to buy food.*

Or, in more natural English:
> *The woman sent a slave to buy food.*

You have also met purpose clauses used with **ubi**:

> locum quaerēbāmus **ubi stārēmus**.
> *We were looking for a place where we might stand.*

Or, in more natural English:
> *We were looking for a place to stand.*

3 Further examples:

a sacerdōs haruspicem arcessīvit quī victimam īnspiceret.
b lībertus dōnum quaerēbat quod patrōnum dēlectāret.
c Haterius quīnque fabrōs ēlēgit quī figūrās in arcū sculperent.
d domum emere volēbam ubi fīlius meus habitāret.
e senātor gemmam pretiōsam ēmit quam uxōrī daret.
f fēminae līberīque locum invēnērunt ubi latērent.

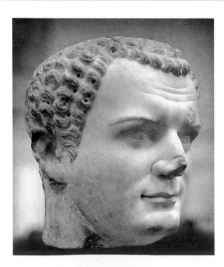

The Emperor Titus was enormously popular but reigned only three years.

Word patterns: compound verbs 1

1 Study the following verbs and their translations:

currere	dēcurrere	excurrere	recurrere
to run	*to run down*	*to run out*	*to run back*

iacere	dēicere	ēicere	reicere
to throw	*to throw down*	*to throw out*	*to throw back*

2 Verbs may have their meaning extended by placing **dē**, **ex** or **re** at the beginning of the word. Such verbs are known as compound verbs.

3 Using the pattern above, complete the following table:

trahere	dētrahere	extrahere	retrahere
to pull, drag	. . . .	. . . .	. . . .

cadere	dēcidere	excidere	recidere
to fall	. . . .	. . . .	. . . .

mittere	. . . .	ēmittere	. . . .
to send	. . . .	. . . .	. . . .

4 Complete the following sentences with the correct compound verb. Then translate the sentences.

> dēpōnerent   ēdūcēbantur   revēnērunt

  a fabrī, postquam domum . . . ., diū dormīvērunt.
  b lēgātus hostibus imperāvit ut arma . . . .
  c mīlitēs ē castrīs . . . . ut rūpem Masadam oppugnārent.

5 Explain the connection between the following Latin verbs and the English verbs derived from them.

dēpōnere	*depose*	ērumpere	*erupt*	retinēre	*retain*
dēspicere	*despise*	ēicere	*eject*	referre	*refer*

Practising the language

1 Complete each sentence with the right form of the imperfect subjunctive, using the verb in brackets. Then translate the sentence.

For example: Domitiānus ad āram prōcessit ut victimam . . . . (sacrificāre)
Answer: Domitiānus ad āram prōcessit ut victimam **sacrificāret**.
Domitian advanced to the altar in order to sacrifice the victim.

The forms of the imperfect subjunctive are given on p. 128.

a equitēs īnsidiās parāvērunt ut ducem hostium . . . . (capere)
b ad forum contendēbāmus ut pompam . . . . (spectāre)
c barbarī facēs in manibus tenēbant ut templum . . . . (incendere)
d extrā carcerem stābam ut captīvōs . . . . (custōdīre)
e Haterī, quam strēnuē labōrāvistī ut arcum . . . . ! (perficere)
f rūpem Masadam occupāvimus ut Rōmānīs . . . . (resistere)

2 Complete each sentence with the most suitable participle from the lists below, using the correct form. Then translate the sentence. Do not use any participle more than once.

dūcēns	labōrāns	sedēns	incēdēns	clāmāns
dūcentem	labōrantem	sedentem	incēdentem	clāmantem
dūcentēs	labōrantēs	sedentēs	incēdentēs	clāmantēs

a videō Salvium prope arcum . . . .
b fabrī, in Viā Sacrā . . . ., valdē fessī erant.
c nōnne audīs puerōs . . . .?
d iuvenis, victimam . . . ., ārae appropinquāvit.
e spectātōrēs captīvōs, per viās . . . ., dērīdēbant.

3 Translate each English sentence into Latin by selecting correctly from the list of Latin words.

a *The citizens, having been delighted by the show, applauded.*

| cīvis | spectāculum | dēlectātī | plaudunt |
| cīvēs | spectāculō | dēlectātus | plausērunt |

b *I recognised the slave-girl who was pouring the wine.*

| ancilla | quī | vīnum | fundēbat | agnōvī |
| ancillam | quae | vīnō | fundēbant | agnōvit |

c *Having returned to the bank of the river, the soldiers halted.*

| ad rīpam | flūmine | regressī | mīlitēs | cōnstitērunt |
| ad rīpās | flūminis | regressōs | mīlitum | cōnstiterant |

d *The woman, sitting in prison, told a sad story.*

| fēmina | in carcerem | sedēns | fābulam | trīstis | nārrat |
| fēminae | in carcere | sedentem | fābulae | trīstem | nārrāvit |

e *We saw the altar, decorated with flowers.*

| āram | flōrī | ōrnāta | vīdī |
| ārās | flōribus | ōrnātam | vīdimus |

f *They killed the sleeping prisoners with swords.*

| captīvī | dormientem | gladiōs | occīdērunt |
| captīvōs | dormientēs | gladiīs | occīdit |

The arch of Titus, looking towards the Forum.

The Roman Forum

The Forum of Rome (**Forum Rōmānum**) was not only the social and commercial centre of the city; it was the centre of the whole empire. To symbolise this, the Emperor Augustus placed a golden milestone (**mīliārium aureum**) in the Forum to mark the starting-point of the roads that radiated from the city to all the corners of the empire.

The ordinary people of Rome came in great numbers to the Forum, sometimes to visit its temples and public buildings, sometimes to listen to speeches or watch a procession, and sometimes just to meet friends and stroll about, pausing at times to gossip, listen to an argument, or bargain with a passing street-trader.

In the **basilicae** (3, 7), lawyers pleaded their cases in front of large and often noisy audiences, and merchants and bankers negotiated their business deals. Senators made their way to the **cūria** or senate-house (8) to conduct the affairs of government under the leadership of the emperor. Sometimes a funeral procession wound its way through the Forum, accompanied by noisy lamentations and loud music; sometimes the crowd was forced to make way for a wealthy noble as he was carried through the Forum in a litter by his slaves and escorted by a long line of citizens.

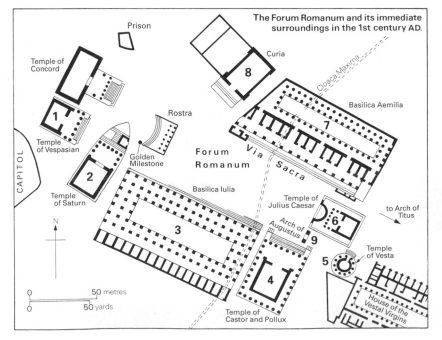

Above: *The Forum Romanum seen from the Palatine Hill.*
1, 2 Columns belonging to the temples of Vespasian and Saturn;
3 Corner of the Basilica Iulia;
4 Base and three columns of the temple of Castor and Pollux;
5 Remains of the temple of Vesta;
6 Foundations of the temple of Julius Caesar;
7 A white archway leading into the Basilica Aemilia;
8 Curia. Near it is the arch of Severus built in the 3rd century AD.

Right: *A reconstruction of the Forum looking the opposite way to the photograph, towards the Palatine Hill:*
6 Temple of Julius Caesar;
9 Arch of Augustus;
4 Temple of Castor and Pollux;
3 Basilica Iulia.
The columns with statues on top were built in the 4th century AD.

The Forum lay on low ground between two of Rome's hills, the Capitol and the Palatine. On the Capitol at the western end of the Forum stood the temple of Jupiter Optimus Maximus, the centre of the Roman state religion. This was where the emperor came to pray for the continued safety of the Roman people; and this was where the consuls took their solemn vows on January 1st each year at the beginning of their consulship. On the Palatine stood the emperor's residence. In the time of Augustus, this had been a relatively modest house; later emperors built palaces of steadily increasing splendour.

Near the foot of the Capitol stood the Rostra, a platform from which public speeches were made to the people. It took its name from the **rōstra** (ships' prows) which had been captured in a sea battle early in Rome's history and were used to decorate it. One of the most famous speeches made from the Rostra was Mark Antony's speech over the body of Julius Caesar in 44 BC. The listening crowds were so carried away by Antony's words and so angry at Caesar's murder that they rioted, seized the body, and burned it in the Forum. A temple was later built in Caesar's memory at the eastern end of the Forum (6), on the spot where his body had been burned.

Not far from the Rostra was the prison. Prisoners of war, like the seven Jews in the stories of this Stage, were held in the prison before being led in a triumphal procession through the streets of Rome. Afterwards they were taken back to the prison and killed.

Just outside the Forum, near the temple of the deified Julius Caesar, was a small round building with a cone-shaped roof. This was the temple of Vesta (5), where the Vestal Virgins tended the sacred fire which symbolised the prosperity of Rome and was never allowed to go out.

Through the Forum ran the Sacred Way (**Via Sacra**), which provided an avenue for religious or triumphal processions. When the Romans celebrated a victory in war, the triumphal procession passed through the city and ended by travelling along the Sacred Way towards the temple of Jupiter on the Capitol, where the victorious general gave thanks. The story on pp. 9–10 describes a similar occasion: the dedication of the arch of Titus by the Emperor Domitian in AD 81. On this occasion, the procession would have followed the Sacred Way eastwards out of the Forum, up a gentle slope to the site of the arch itself. The arch commemorated the victory of Domitian's brother Titus over the Jewish people.

The Forum Romanum was not the only forum in the city. By the time of the events of this Stage, three other forums had been built by Julius Caesar, Augustus and Vespasian; later, two more were added by the Emperors Nerva and Trajan. The most splendid of these was Trajan's forum, which contained the famous column commemorating Trajan's victories over the

The prison. Once a cistern for storing water, this cell was entered through a hole in the roof.

The temple of Vesta.

The Sacred Way winding up to the arch of Titus.

Dacians. But none of these other forums replaced the Forum Romanum as the political, religious and social heart of the city. If one Roman said to another, 'I'll meet you in the Forum', he meant the Forum Romanum.

The Jews and the Romans

Judaea, now part of modern Israel, became a Roman province early in the first century AD. The Jews were a fiercely independent people and sometimes were unwilling to tolerate Roman rule. In particular, they could be angered by what they saw as the lack of respect shown by the Romans for their religion. The Romans, in turn, could not understand a people who insisted that there was only one true God and who would not acknowledge the claims of any other religion. The situation was made worse by the incompetence of Roman governors and quarrelling among different sections of the Jewish population.

In AD 66 a serious rebellion broke out, which raged for four years before it ended with the capture of Jerusalem by Titus, son of the Emperor Vespasian. His soldiers slaughtered an enormous number of Jews; they sacked the city and destroyed the Temple, the Jews' most sacred shrine. In an attempt to prevent any future rebellion, many of the survivors were driven out of the country and scattered. Titus returned to Rome with prisoners and the Temple treasure to celebrate a triumph with his father.

However, Jewish resistance had not completely ended. A group of fervent patriots, the Zealots, led by Eleazar ben Ya'ir, had established themselves at Masada, a fortress on a high flat-topped hill near the Dead Sea. From this base they harassed the Roman occupation forces for two years until in AD 72 the commander of the Tenth Legion, Flavius Silva, determined to wipe them out.

The story of the last days of Masada which is told on pp. 6–7 is based on the account given by the historian Josephus. He may have talked to eye-witnesses and may even have questioned the two women and the children who had hidden underground and who subsequently surrendered to the Roman soldiers.

In 1963–5 the site of Masada was excavated by a team of archaeologists led by Yigael Yadin. They have brought to light much evidence of the last days of Eleazar and his companions.

One of the most exciting finds was a group of eleven small pottery fragments, each bearing a single name, and unlike any others found on the site. One has 'ben Ya'ir' written on it and it is

Above: *A synagogue at Masada.*
Below: *A room in a Roman-style bath house at Masada, showing some of the hypocaust pillars and wall flue bricks.*

thought that this may refer to Eleazar. It is tempting to connect the fragments to the lots that were drawn by the Jewish defenders, but there is no firm evidence to support this.

Titus succeeded Vespasian as emperor in AD 79 but died three years later. To commemorate his brother's victory over the Jews, Domitian dedicated a triumphal arch in the Forum some time after his death. The story about the procession is fictitious (nothing is known about the fate of Simon and his family), but it is possible that the temple treasures, which are shown on the arch, were again paraded through the streets of Rome. They remained in Rome until the city was sacked by the Vandals in the fifth century. What happened to them after that remains a mystery.

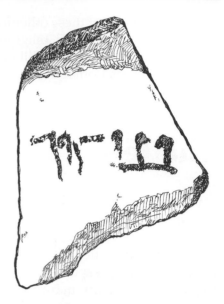

Above: *The piece of pottery with the name ben Ya'ir.*
Below: *Silva's headquarters camp, one of five Roman camps surrounding the rock.*

The rock of Masada seen from the north. The Roman ramp can be clearly seen rising from the right. The western palace on the right of the ramp and the northern palace on the left were built by Herod the Great a century before the Roman siege in AD 72–3.

Vocabulary checklist 29

aliī … aliī	*some … others*
ascendō, ascendere, ascendī	*climb, rise*
audācia, audāciae	*boldness, audacity*
captīvus, captīvī	*prisoner, captive*
circumveniō, circumvenīre, circumvēnī, circumventus	*surround*
dēfendō, dēfendere, dēfendī, dēfēnsus	*defend*
dīrus, dīra, dīrum	*dreadful*
dolor, dolōris	*grief, pain*
incēdō, incēdere, incessī	*march, stride*
līberī, līberōrum	*children*
lūx, lūcis	*light, daylight*
mālō, mālle, māluī	*prefer*
ōdī	*I hate*
perficiō, perficere, perfēcī, perfectus	*finish*
populus, populī	*people*
prius	*earlier*
salūs, salūtis	*safety, health*
scelus, sceleris	*crime*
spernō, spernere, sprēvī, sprētus	*despise, reject*
ubīque	*everywhere*
vester, vestra, vestrum	*your (plural)*
vīvus, vīva, vīvum	*alive, living*

A coin (much enlarged), issued in AD 71, of the Emperor Vespasian, celebrating the defeat of the Jews. A victorious prince stands to the left of the palm. A Jewish captive sits on the right.

HATERIUS

STAGE 30

cotīdiē cīvēs ad arcum conveniēbant ut figūrās in eō sculptās īnspicerent.

1 Haterius: quam fēlīx sum!
           heri arcus meus ab Imperātōre dēdicātus est.
           heri praemium ingēns mihi ā Salviō prōmissum est.
           hodiē praemium exspectō ...

2 Haterius: anxius sum.
           arcus meus nūper ab Imperātōre laudātus est.
           nūllum tamen praemium adhūc mihi ā Salviō
           missum est.
           num ego ā Salviō dēceptus sum?
           minimē! Salvius vir probus est ...

dignitās

When you have read this story, answer the questions at the end.

cīvēs Rōmānī, postquam arcus ab Imperātōre dēdicātus est, quattuor diēs fēstōs celebrāvērunt. cotīdiē ad arcum conveniēbant ut figūrās in eō sculptās īnspicerent. plūrimī clientēs domum Salviī veniēbant quī grātulātiōnēs eī facerent. Salvius ipse summō gaudiō affectus est quod Imperātor arcum Hateriī magnopere laudāverat.

apud Haterium tamen nūllae grātulantium vōcēs audītae sunt. neque clientēs neque amīcī admissī sunt. Haterius, īrā commōtus, sōlus domī manēbat. adeō saeviēbat ut dormīre nōn posset. quattuor diēs noctēsque vigilābat. quīntō diē uxor, Vitellia nōmine, quae nesciēbat quārē Haterius adeō īrātus esset, eum mollīre temptābat. ingressa hortum, ubi Haterius hūc illūc ambulābat, eum anxia interrogāvit.

Vitellia:	cūr tam vehementer saevīs, mī Haterī? et amīcōs et clientēs, quī vēnērunt ut tē salūtārent, domō abēgistī. neque ūnum verbum mihi hōs quattuor diēs dīxistī. sine dubiō, ut istum arcum cōnficerēs, nimis labōrāvistī, neglegēns valētūdinis tuae. nunc necesse est tibi quiēscere.
Haterius:	quō modō ego, tantam iniūriam passus, quiēscere possum?
Vitellia:	verba tua nōn intellegō. quis tibi iniūriam intulit?
Haterius:	ego ā Salviō, quī mihi favēre solēbat, omnīnō dēceptus sum. prō omnibus meīs labōribus ingēns praemium mihi ā Salviō prōmissum est. nūllum praemium tamen, nē grātiās quidem, accēpī.
Vitellia:	contentus estō, mī Haterī! redēmptor nōtissimus es, cuius arcus ab Imperātōre ipsō nūper laudātus est. multa aedificia pūblica exstrūxistī, unde magnās dīvitiās comparāvistī.
Haterius:	dīvitiās nōn cūrō. in hāc urbe sunt plūrimī redēmptōrēs quī opēs maximās comparāvērunt. mihi autem nōn dīvitiae sed dignitās est cūrae.
Vitellia:	dignitās tua amplissima est. nam nōn modo dītissimus es sed etiam uxōrem nōbilissimā gente nātam habēs. Rūfilla, soror mea, uxor est Salviī quī tibi semper fāvit et saepe tē Imperātōrī commendāvit. quid aliud ā Salviō accipere cupis?
Haterius:	volō ad summōs honōrēs pervenīre. prīmum sacerdōs esse cupiō; multī enim virī, sacerdōtēs ab Imperātōre creātī, posteā ad cōnsulātum pervēnērunt. sed Salvius, quamquam sacerdōtium

clientēs: cliēns *client*
grātulātiōnēs: grātulātiō *congratulation*
gaudiō: gaudium *joy*
grātulantium: grātulāns *congratulating*
vigilābat: vigilāre *stay awake*
quīntō: quīntus *fifth*
hūc illūc *here and there, up and down*

abēgistī: abigere *drive away*

valētūdinis: valētūdō *health*

nē ... quidem *not even*
estō! *be!*

pūblica: pūblicus *public*
dīvitiās: dīvitiae *riches*

est cūrae *is a matter of concern*
amplissima: amplissimus *very great*
dītissimus: dīves *rich*

commendāvit: commendāre *recommend*
cōnsulātum: cōnsulātus *consulship (rank of consul)*
sacerdōtium *priesthood*

Vitellia: mihi identidem prōmīsit, fidem nōn servāvit.
nōlī dēspērāre, mī Haterī! cōnsilium optimum
habeō. invītā Salvium ad āream tuam! ostentā eī   45
polyspaston tuum! nihil maius nec mīrābilius
umquam anteā factum est. deinde Salvium
admīrātiōne affectum rogā dē sacerdōtiō.

fidem ... servāvit: fidem
  servāre *keep a promise, keep
  faith*
āream: ārea *builder's yard*
ostentā: ostentāre *show off,
  display*
nec *nor*

Questions

		Marks
1	How long was the holiday that followed the dedication of the arch?	1
2	Describe the scene at the arch during the holiday (lines 2–3)	2
3	Why did Salvius' clients come to his house?	1
4	**Salvius ... gaudiō affectus est** (line 5). What was the reason for this?	1
5	What happened to Haterius' friends and clients (line 8)?	1
6	Haterius' feelings were very different from those of Salvius. Pick out a Latin phrase or verb that tells you how he was feeling (lines 8–10).	1
7	How did Vitellia behave towards her husband (lines 10–12)?	1
8	What did she think was the matter with Haterius (lines 17–18)?	1
9	What remedy did she suggest?	1
10	In what way did Haterius think he had been deceived (lines 23–6)?	3
11	Vitellia urged Haterius to be content with his achievements. Give two that she mentioned.	2
12	**dīvitiās nōn cūrō** (line 31). What did Haterius really want?	1
13	**uxōrem nōbilissimā gente nātam habēs** (lines 35–6). Explain how Vitellia's family connections have brought Haterius special benefits.	3
14	What particular honour did Haterius want to receive first? What did he hope it would lead to (lines 39–42)?	2
15	What actions did Vitellia suggest to Haterius? How did she think her plan would help Haterius to get what he wanted (lines 45–8)?	2 + 2

TOTAL **25**

About the language 1: perfect passive tense

1 In this Stage, you have met the perfect passive. Compare it with the perfect active:

perfect active
senex fūrem **accūsāvit**.
*The old man **has accused** the thief.*
Or,
*The old man **accused** the thief.*

perfect passive
fūr ā sene **accūsātus est**.
*The thief **has been accused** by the old man.*
Or,
*The thief **was accused** by the old man.*

Rōmānī hostēs **superāvērunt**.
*The Romans **have overcome** the enemy.*
Or,
*The Romans **overcame** the enemy.*

hostēs ā Rōmānīs **superātī sunt**.
*The enemy **have been overcome** by the Romans.*
Or,
*The enemy **were overcome** by the Romans.*

2 The forms of the perfect passive are as follows:

SINGULAR
portātus sum   *I have been carried*, or *I was carried*
portātus es   *you (s.) have been carried*, or *you were carried*
portātus est   *he has been carried*, or *he was carried*

PLURAL
portātī sumus   *we have been carried*, or *we were carried*
portātī estis   *you (pl.) have been carried*, or *you were carried*
portātī sunt   *they have been carried*, or *they were carried*

3 Notice that each form of the perfect passive is made up of two words:

a a perfect passive participle (e.g. **portātus**) in either a singular or a plural form;
b a form of the present tense of **sum**.

4 Further examples:

a arcus ab Imperātōre dēdicātus est.
b multī nūntiī ad urbem missī sunt.
c dux hostium ā mīlitibus captus est.
d cūr ad vīllam nōn invītātī estis?
e ā Salviō dēceptus sum.
f audītus est; monitī sumus; laudātus es; interfectī sunt.

5 If **inventus est** means *he was found*, what do you think **inventa est** means?

polyspaston

I

postrīdiē Haterius Salvium ad āream suam dūxit ut polyspaston
eī ostentāret. ibi sedēbat ōtiōsus Glitus, magister fabrōrum. quī
cum dominum appropinquantem cōnspexisset, celeriter surrēxit
fabrōsque dīligentius labōrāre iussit.

tōta ārea strepitū labōrantium plēna erat. columnae ex   *5*
marmore pretiōsissimō secābantur; laterēs saxaque in āream
portābantur; ingentēs marmoris massae in plaustra pōnēbantur.
Haterius, cum fabrōs labōre occupātōs vīdisset, Salvium ad
aliam āreae partem dūxit. ibi stābat ingēns polyspaston quod ā
fabrīs parātum erat. in tignō polyspastī sēdēs fīxa erat. tum   *10*
Haterius ad Salvium versus,

'mī Salvī', inquit, 'nōnne mīrābile est polyspaston? hoc tibi
tālem urbis prōspectum praebēre potest quālem paucī umquam
vīdērunt. placetne tibi?'

Salvius, ubi sēdem in tignō fīxam vīdit, palluit. sed, quia fabrī *15*
oculōs in eum dēfīxōs habēbant, timōrem dissimulāns in sēdem
cōnsēdit. iuxtā eum Haterius quoque cōnsēdit. tum fabrīs
imperāvit ut fūnēs, quī ad tignum adligātī erant, summīs vīribus
traherent. deinde tignum lentē ad caelum tollēbātur. Salvius,
pavōre paene cōnfectus, clausīs oculīs ad sēdem haerēbat.   *20*
tandem oculōs aperuit.

dīligentius *more diligently,*
  harder
laterēs: later *brick*

tignō: tignum *beam*
sēdēs *seat*
fīxa erat: fīgere *fix, fasten*
tālem … quālem *such … as*
prōspectum: prōspectus *view*
quia *because*
timōrem: timor *fear*
dissimulāns: dissimulāre
  conceal, hide
iuxtā *next to*
fūnēs: fūnis *rope*
adligātī erant: adligāre *tie*
vīribus: vīrēs *strength*

Haterius and his crane.

II

Salvius:	*(spectāculō attonitus)* dī immortālēs! tōtam urbem vidēre possum. ecce templum Iovis! ecce flūmen! ecce amphitheātrum Flāvium et arcus novus! quam in sōle fulget! Imperātor, simulatque illum arcum vīdit, summā admīrātiōne affectus est. mihi imperāvit ut grātiās suās tibi agerem.
Haterius:	magnopere gaudeō quod opus meum ab Imperātōre laudātum est. sed praemium illud quod tū mihi prōmīsistī nōndum accēpī.
Salvius	*(vōce blandā)* dē sacerdōtiō tuō, Imperātōrem iam saepe cōnsuluī, et respōnsum eius etiam nunc exspectō. aliquid tamen tibi intereā offerre possum. agellum quendam possideō, quī prope sepulcra Metellōrum et Scīpiōnum situs est. tūne hunc agellum emere velīs?
Haterius:	*(magnō gaudiō affectus)* ita vērō, in illō agellō, prope sepulcra gentium nōbilissimārum, ego quoque sepulcrum splendidum mihi meīsque exstruere velim, figūrīs operum meōrum ōrnātum; ita enim nōmen factaque mea posterīs trādere possum. prō agellō tuō igitur sēstertium vīciēns tibi offerō.
Salvius:	*(rīdēns, quod agellus eī grātīs ab Imperātōre datus erat)* agellus multō plūris est, sed quia patrōnus sum tuus tibi faveō. mē iuvat igitur sēstertium tantum trīciēns ā tē accipere. placetne tibi?
Haterius:	mihi valdē placet.

Haterius fabrīs imperāvit ut tignum lentē dēmitterent. ambō humum rediērunt, alter spē immortālitātis dēlectātus, alter praesentī pecūniā contentus.

5

10

15

20

25

Iovis: Iuppiter *Jupiter (god of the sky, greatest of Roman gods)*
amphitheātrum Flāvium *Flavian amphitheatre (now known as the Colosseum)*
nōndum *not yet*
agellum: agellus *small plot of land*
quendam: quīdam *one, a certain*
sepulcra: sepulcrum *tomb*
Metellōrum: Metellī *the Metelli (famous Roman family)*
Scīpiōnum: Scīpiōnēs *the Scipiones (famous Roman family)*
meīs: meī *my family*
facta: factum *deed, achievement*
posterīs: posterī *future generations, posterity*
sēstertium vīciēns *two million sesterces*
multō plūris est *is worth much more*
mē iuvat *it pleases me*
sēstertium … trīciēns *three million sesterces*
humum *to the ground*
immortālitātis: immortālitās *immortality*
praesentī: praesēns *present, ready*

These two portraits, from the tomb of the Haterii, could represent Haterius and his wife.

About the language 2: pluperfect passive tense

1   You have now met the pluperfect passive. Compare it with the pluperfect active:

pluperfect active
servus dominum **vulnerāverat**.
*A slave **had wounded** the master.*

pluperfect passive
dominus ā servō **vulnerātus erat**.
*The master **had been wounded** by a slave.*

2   The forms of the pluperfect passive are as follows:

SINGULAR
portātus eram   *I had been carried*
portātus erās   *you (s.) had been carried*
portātus erat   *he had been carried*

PLURAL
portātī erāmus   *we had been carried*
portātī erātis   *you (pl.) had been carried*
portātī erant   *they had been carried*

Each form of the pluperfect passive is made up of a perfect passive participle (e.g. **portātus**) and a form of the imperfect tense of **sum** (e.g. **erat**).

3   Further examples:

a   Simōn ā mātre servātus erat.
b   custōdēs circum carcerem positī erant.
c   dīligenter labōrāre iussī erātis.
d   ā mīlitibus Rōmānīs superātī erāmus.
e   fēmina ā filiō vituperāta erat.
f   pūnīta erat; pūnītae erant; missus eram; audītae erāmus; victus erās.

Word patterns: adjectives and nouns

1   Study the form and meaning of the following adjectives and nouns:

probus	*honest*	probitās	*honesty*
līber	*free*	lībertās	*freedom*
gravis	*heavy, serious*	gravitās	*heaviness, seriousness*

2   Now complete the table below:

benignus	*kind*	benignitās	. . . .
līberālis	. . . .	līberālitās	*generosity*
fēlīx	*lucky, happy*	fēlīcitās	. . . .
celer	. . . .	celeritās	*speed*
immortālis	. . . .	immortālitās	. . . .
suāvis	. . . .	. . . .	. . . .

3   Give the meaning of the following nouns:

   crūdēlitās, tranquillitās, calliditās, paupertās.

4   How many of the nouns in paragraphs 1–3 can be translated by an English derivative ending in *-ity* or *-ty*? Use an English dictionary to help you, if necessary.

A Roman architect or contractor, holding a measuring stick. On the right (from top) are a chisel, a plumb-line, a set-square and the capital of a column; on the left, a stonemason's hammer.

Practising the language

1   Translate the following sentences. After each one state whether the verb is present or imperfect and whether it is active or passive.

   a   populus Rōmānus Titum maximē dīligēbat.
   b   fabrī ab Hateriō tōtam noctem incitābantur.
   c   hodiē cēna splendida Imperātōrī parātur.
   d   quattuor diēs ingēns multitūdō viās urbis complēbat.
   e   magnus strepitus in āreā audiēbātur.
   f   pauperēs ā dīvitibus saepe opprimuntur.

2   Complete each sentence with the right word. Then translate the sentence.

   a   mercātor, ē carcere . . . ., magistrātuī grātiās ēgit. (līberātus, līberātī)
   b   māter, verbīs Eleazārī . . . ., cum līberīs latēbat. (territus, territa)
   c   Salvius epistulam, ab Imperātōre . . . ., legēbat. (scrīpta, scrīptam)
   d   nāvēs, tempestāte paene . . . ., tandem ad portum revēnērunt.
       (dēlētus, dēlēta, dēlētae)
   e   centuriō captīvōs, ā mīlitibus . . . ., in castra dūxit. (custōdītī,
       custōdītōs, custōdītīs)

3   Complete each sentence with the most suitable ending of the pluperfect subjunctive. Then translate the sentence.

   For example: cum hospitēs advēn…, coquus cēnam intulit.
   This becomes: cum hospitēs **advēnissent**, coquus cēnam intulit.
                  When the guests had arrived, the cook brought the dinner in.

   The forms of the pluperfect subjunctive are given on p. 128.

   a   cum servus iānuam aperu… . senex intrāvit.
   b   cum pompam spectāv…, ad arcum festīnāvī.
   c   Imperātor nōs rogāvit num arcum īnspex… .
   d   cum Rōmam vīsitāv…, domum rediistis?
   e   amīcī nōn intellēxērunt cūr Haterium nōn vīd… .

Roman builders

The various carvings on the family tomb of the Haterii, especially the crane, suggest that at least one member of the family was a prosperous building contractor. His personal names are unknown but in the stories we have called him Quintus Haterius Latronianus. One of his contracts may have been for a magnificent arch to commemorate the popular Emperor Titus who died after only a short reign (AD 79–81). In Stage 29, Haterius is imagined as anxiously trying to complete it during the night before its dedication by the new emperor, Domitian, and in this Stage he is seeking his reward.

Helped by an architect who provided the design and technical advice Haterius would have employed sub-contractors to supply the materials and engage the workmen. Most of these were slaves and poor free men working as unskilled, occasional labour, but there were also craftsmen such as carpenters and stonemasons. It was the job of the carpenters to put up a timber framework to give shape and temporary support to the arches as they were being built (see diagram alongside). They also erected the scaffolding and made the timber moulds for shaping concrete. The masons were responsible for quarrying the stone and transporting it, often by barge on the river Tiber, to the building-site in the city before carving the elaborate decoration and preparing the blocks to be lifted into position. The richly carved panels on Titus' arch showed the triumphal procession with prisoners and treasure captured at the sack of Jerusalem in AD 70.

Roman architecture depended on good quality cement. The main ingredients of this versatile and easily produced material were:

1 lime, made by heating pieces of limestone to a high temperature and then crushing them to a powder;
2 fine river or quarry sand.

These were combined with water to make a smooth paste. In this form the cement was an excellent adhesive which could be spread in a thin layer between bricks or stones, as we do today, and when dry it held them firmly together.

The Romans also mixed cement with rubble, such as stone chippings, broken bricks and pieces of tile, to form concrete. Concrete was commonly used for the inner core of a wall, sandwiched between the two faces. The advantage of this was that the more expensive materials, good quality stone or brick, could be reserved for the outer faces; these were often then covered with plaster and painted in bright colours. Marble too, in thinly cut plates, was used as a facing material where cost was no object.

Wooden 'centring' supporting the stones of an arch. Once the central 'keystone' was in place, the arch could support itself and the wood was removed.

Haterius' crane

There is a crane carved on the tomb of Haterius' family. It consisted of two wooden uprights, forming the jib, fastened together at the top and splayed apart at the feet. The hoisting rope ran round two pulleys, one at the top of the jib and one at the point where the load was fastened to the rope. After passing round the pulleys the rope led down to a winding drum, which was turned by a treadmill fixed to the side of the crane and operated by two or three men inside. Smaller cranes had, instead of the treadmill, a capstan with projecting spokes to be turned by hand. This arrangement of pulleys and ropes multiplied the force exerted by human muscles so that a small crew could raise loads weighing up to eight or nine tonnes. To prevent the crane from toppling over, stay-ropes were stretched out from the jib, also with the help of pulleys, and firmly anchored to the ground.

Blocks of dressed stone were lifted by man-powered cranes like this. These machines were certainly cumbersome, but with a skilled crew in charge they worked well.

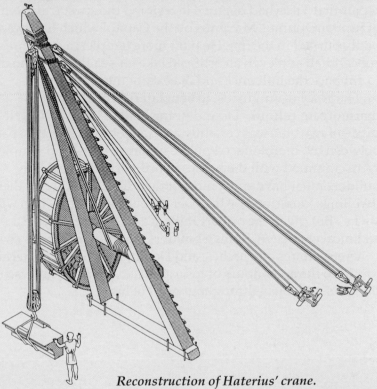

Reconstruction of Haterius' crane.

The Romans discovered a further use for concrete, substituting it for stone in the building of arches, vaulted ceilings and domes. They found that concrete, when shaped into arches, was strong enough to span large spaces without any additional support from pillars, and that it could carry the weight of a heavy superstructure. They used it, for instance, on the aqueducts that supplied Rome with millions of litres of fresh water daily; they also used it on the Pantheon, a temple whose domed concrete and brick roof (still in good condition today) has a span of 43 metres and rises to the same height above the floor. Most spectacularly of all, they also used it on the huge Flavian amphitheatre (known from medieval times as the Colosseum), which could hold about 50,000 spectators, and may be another of Haterius' surviving buildings (see opposite page).

Not all buildings, of course, were so well constructed. The inhabitants of Rome in the first century AD were housed in a vast number of dwellings, many of them blocks of flats (**īnsulae**) which were built cheaply, mainly of brick and timber. They had a reputation for being rickety and liable to catch fire. To reduce the danger the Emperor Augustus fixed a limit of 21 metres in height for these insulae and organised fire brigades. Further regulations followed the great fire of Rome in the reign of Nero.

However, serious fires continued to break out from time to time. One occurred in AD 80 and when Domitian became emperor in the following year he continued the programme of repair that Titus had begun. He restored the spectacular temple of Jupiter Optimus Maximus on the Capitol which had been badly burned in the fire. He built more temples, a stadium, a concert hall and even an artificial lake for sea fights, all no doubt to enhance the influence and majesty of the emperor.

The boast of Augustus, **urbem latericiam accēpī, marmoream relīquī**, 'I found Rome built of brick and left it made of marble', was certainly an exaggeration. For the spaces between the marble-faced public libraries, baths and temples were crammed with the homes of ordinary people. Many builders must have spent most of their time working on these dwellings, described by the poet Juvenal as 'propped up with sticks'. But given the opportunity of a large contract and a technical challenge, Roman builders made adventurous use of concrete, cranes and arches; and Domitian, who was determined to add to the splendours of his capital city, kept architects and builders very busy throughout most of his reign.

Concrete

The Romans were not the first people to make concrete – rubble set in mortar – but they improved its quality and applied it on a grand scale.

A Roman trowel from Verulamium (St Albans) in Britain, left by mistake in some concrete. Many of our modern hand tools have been inherited almost unchanged from those used by Roman craftsmen.

Left: *The Romans often built walls out of concrete sandwiched between two surfaces of brick or small stones – as we can see at the back of this room in a public baths. In the centre there is a piece of wall coming towards us, with the surface stones visible at each side of it. These concrete walls would have been hidden by marble sheets or painted plaster, so that they looked as rich as the coloured marble columns and the mosaic floor.*

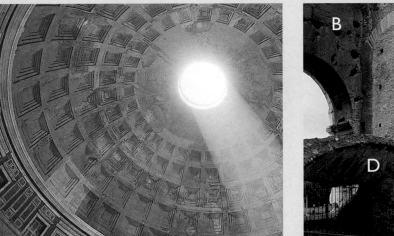

Concrete was used to span large spaces. This is the dome of the Pantheon.

Top: *Concrete was used alongside other building materials, as in the Colosseum. On the outside the amphitheatre appears to be all stone.*
Bottom: *Inside we find a mixture of stone walls (A and B), walls made of brick-faced concrete (C) and concrete vaulting (D).*

Vocabulary checklist 30

adhūc	*up till now*
afficiō, afficere, affēcī, affectus	*affect*
affectus, affecta, affectum	*affected, overcome*
ambō, ambae, ambō	*both*
cōnsulō, cōnsulere, cōnsuluī,	
cōnsultus	*consult*
dēmittō, dēmittere, dēmīsī,	
dēmissus	*let down, lower*
dīves, *gen.* dīvitis	*rich*
dīvitiae, dīvitiārum	*riches*
gēns, gentis	*family, tribe*
iniūria, iniūriae	*injustice, injury*
magnopere	*greatly*
nātus, nāta, nātum	*born*
nimis	*too*
nōbilis, nōbile	*noble, of noble birth*
omnīnō	*completely*
opus, operis	*work, construction*
pavor, pavōris	*panic*
quārē?	*why?*
saxum, saxī	*rock*
secō, secāre, secuī, sectus	*cut*
sōl, sōlis	*sun*
soror, sorōris	*sister*
timor, timōris	*fear*

Stamp cut from a Roman brick. Bricks were often stamped with the date and place of manufacture.

IN URBE

STAGE 31

1   diēs illūcēscēbat.

2   diē illūcēscente, multī saccāriī in rīpā flūminis labōrābant.

3   saccāriīs labōrantibus, advēnit nāvis. nautae nāvem dēligāvērunt.

4   nāve dēligātā, saccāriī frūmentum expōnere coepērunt.

5 frūmentō expositō, magister nāvis
  pecūniam saccāriīs distribuit.

6 pecūniā distribūtā, saccāriī ad tabernam
  proximam festīnāvērunt.

7 tandem sōl occidere coepit.

8 sōle occidente, saccāriī ā tabernā ēbriī
  discessērunt, omnī pecūniā cōnsūmptā.

Īnsula Tiberīna

adventus

diē illūcēscente, ingēns Rōmānōrum multitūdō viās urbis
complēbat. in rīpīs flūminis Tiberis, ubi multa horrea sita erant,
frūmentum ē nāvibus ā saccāriīs expōnēbātur. servī, quī ā
vēnālīciīs ex Āfricā importātī erant, ē nāvibus dūcēbantur,
catēnīs gravibus vīnctī.

    ex ūnā nāvium, quae modo ā Graeciā advēnerat, puella
pulcherrima exiit. epistulam ad Haterium scrīptam manū
tenēbat. sarcinae eius ā servō portābantur, virō quadrāgintā
annōrum.

    sōle ortō, puella ad Subūram advēnit. multitūdine
clāmōribusque hominum valdē obstupefacta est. tanta erat
multitūdō ut puella cum summā difficultāte prōcēderet.
undique pauperēs ex īnsulīs exībant ut aquam ē fontibus
traherent. dīvitēs ad forum lectīcīs vehēbantur. mendīcī puellam
circumveniēbant, pecūniam postulantēs. nōnnūllī fabrī, puellā
vīsā, clāmāre coepērunt; puellam verbīs scurrīlibus
appellāvērunt. quae tamen, clāmōribus fabrōrum neglēctīs,
vultū serēnō celeriter praeteriit. servum iussit festīnāre nē
domum Hateriī tardius pervenīrent.

    eōdem tempore multī clientēs per viās contendēbant ut
patrōnōs salūtārent. aliī, scissīs togīs ruptīsque calceīs, per
lutum lentē ībant. eīs difficile erat festīnāre quia lutum erat
altum, viae angustae, multitūdō dēnsa. aliī, quī nōbilī gente nātī
sunt, celeriter prōcēdēbant quod servī multitūdinem fūstibus
dēmovēbant. clientēs, quī hūc illūc per viās ruēbant, puellae
prōcēdentī obstābant.

illūcēscente: illūcēscere
   dawn, grow bright
Tiberis *river Tiber*
saccāriīs: saccārius *docker,*
   dock-worker
expōnēbātur: expōnere
   unload
catēnīs: catēna *chain*
modo *just*
sarcinae *bags, luggage*
ortō: ortus *having risen*
Subūram: Subūra *the Subura*
   (a noisy and crowded district)
obstupefacta est:
   obstupefacere *amaze, stun*
lectīcīs: lectīca *litter*
mendīcī: mendīcus *beggar*
scurrīlibus: scurrīlis *rude,*
   impudent
appellāvērunt: appellāre *call*
   out to
tardius *too late*
scissīs: scindere *tear*
ruptīs: rumpere *break, split*
lutum *mud*
dēmovēbant: dēmovēre *move*
   out of the way

5

10

15

20

25

A bird's-eye view of Rome

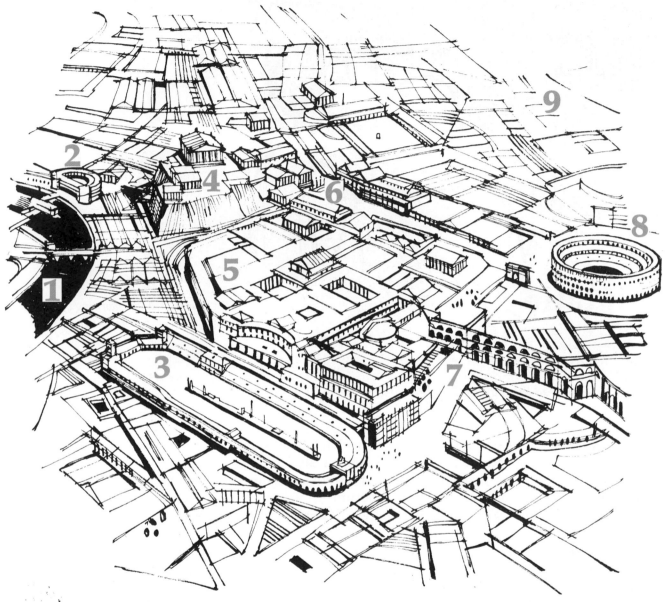

Notice these important features:

1 River Tiber
2 Theatre of Marcellus
3 Circus Maximus, used for chariot racing
4 The Capitol with the temple of Jupiter the Best and Greatest
5 Palatine Hill with the emperor's palace on it
6 Forum Romanum
7 An aqueduct
8 Colosseum or Flavian Amphitheatre
9 Subura.

The drawing shows Rome as it was in the 4th century AD.

salūtātiō

salūtātiō *the morning visit
(made by clients to a patron)*

I

*When you have read this part of the story, answer the questions at
the end.*

prīmā hōrā clientēs ante domum Hateriī conveniēbant. omnēs,
oculīs in iānuā dēfīxīs, patrōnī favōrem exspectābant. aliī
beneficium, aliī sportulam spērābant. puella, servō adstante, in
extrēmā parte multitūdinis cōnstitit; ignāra mōrum
Rōmānōrum, in animō volvēbat cūr tot hominēs illā hōrā ibi   5
stārent.

iānuā subitō apertā, in līmine appāruit praecō. corpus eius
erat ingēns et obēsum, vultus superbus, oculī malignī. clientēs,
praecōne vīsō, clāmāre statim coepērunt. eum identidem
ōrāvērunt ut sē ad patrōnum admitteret. ille tamen superbē   10
circumspectāvit neque quicquam prīmō dīxit.

omnibus tandem silentibus, praecō ita coepit:

'dominus noster, Quīntus Haterius Latrōniānus, ratiōnēs suās
subdūcit. iubet igitur trēs cīvēs ratiōnibus testēs subscrībere.
cēdite C. Iūliō Alexandrō, C. Memmiō Prīmō, L. Venūlēiō   15
Aprōniānō.'

quī igitur, nōminibus suīs audītīs, celeriter prōgressī domum
intrāvērunt. cēterī autem, oculīs in vultū praecōnis dēfīxīs, spē
favōris manēbant.

'ad cēnam', inquit praecō, 'Haterius invītat L. Volusium   20
Maeciānum et M. Licinium Prīvātum. Maeciānus et Prīvātus

---

ante *before, in front of*

sportulam: sportula *handout
(gift of food or money)*
extrēmā parte: extrēma pars
edge
mōrum: mōs *custom*
līmine: līmen *threshold,
doorway*
praecō *herald, announcer*
malignī: malignus *spiteful*
superbē *arrogantly*
ratiōnēs … subdūcit: ratiōnēs
subdūcere *draw up
accounts, write up accounts*
subscrībere *sign*
cēdite: cēdere *make way*

nōnā hōrā redīre iubentur. nunc autem cēdite aliīs! cēdite
architectō C. Rabīriō Maximō! cēdite T. Claudiō Papīriō!'
dum illī per iānuam intrant, cēterīs nūntiāvit praecō:
'vōs omnēs iubet Haterius tertiā hōrā sē ad forum dēdūcere.'   25   **dēdūcere** *escort*
hīs verbīs dictīs, paucōs dēnāriōs in turbam sparsit. clientēs,
nē sportulam āmitterent, dēnāriōs rapere temptāvērunt. inter sē
vehementer certābant. intereā puella immōta stābat, hōc
spectāculō attonita.

Questions

		Marks
1	At what time of day were the clients gathering?	1
2	**omnēs … patrōnī favōrem exspectābant** (lines 1–2). How is this explained further in the next sentence?	2
3	Where did the girl stop?	1
4	What was puzzling her?	2
5	**in līmine appāruit praecō** (line 7). Describe the herald's appearance.	3
6	What did the clients do as soon as they saw him (lines 8–9)?	1
7	What did the clients beg him to do?	1
8	Why do you think the herald remained silent at first (lines 10–11)?	1
9	How can you tell that all the clients mentioned in lines 15–16 are Roman citizens? How can you tell that none of them is a freedman of Haterius?	2
10	When they heard their names why do you think the clients came forward quickly (lines 17–18)?	1
11	What did the rest of the clients do? Why?	2 + 1
12	**ad cēnam … Haterius invītat … M. Licinium Prīvātum** (lines 20–1). Suggest a reason why the herald used this particular order of words.	1
13	**paucōs dēnāriōs in turbam sparsit** (line 26). Why do you think the herald chose this way of distributing the money?	1
14	Re-read the last paragraph and write down two Latin adjectives describing the girl's reaction to the clients' behaviour.	2
15	Look back over lines 13–25. Find two examples of tasks that clients have to perform for their patron and one example of a favour done by patrons to their clients.	2 + 1

TOTAL **25**

II

iānuā tandem clausā, abīre clientēs coepērunt, aliī contentī, aliī
spē dēiectī. deinde servō puella imperāvit ut iānuam pulsāret.
praecōnī regressō servus

    'ecce!' inquit. 'domina mea, Euphrosynē, adest.'

    'abī, sceleste! nēmō alius hodiē admittitur', respondit praecō   5
superbā vōce.

    'sed domina mea est philosopha Graeca doctissima', inquit
servus. 'hūc missa est ā Quīntō Hateriō Chrȳsogonō ipsō,
Hateriī lībertō, quī Athēnīs habitat.'

    'īnsānīvit igitur Chrȳsogonus', respondit praecō. 'odiō sunt   10
omnēs philosophī Hateriō! redeundum vōbīs est Athēnās unde
missī estis.'

    servus arrogantiā praecōnis īrātus, nihilōminus perstitit.

    'sed Eryllus', inquit, 'quī est Hateriō arbiter ēlegantiae,
epistulam ad Chrȳsogonum scrīpsit in quā eum rogāvit ut   15
philosopham hūc mitteret. ergō adsumus!'

    hīs verbīs audītīs, praecō, quī Eryllum haudquāquam
amābat, magnā vōce

    'Eryllus!' inquit. 'quis est Eryllus? meus dominus Haterius
est, nōn Eryllus! abī!'   20

    haec locūtus servum in lutum dēpulit, iānuamque clausit.
Euphrosynē, simulatque servum humī iacentem vīdit, eius īram
lēnīre temptāvit.

    'nōlī', inquit, 'mentem tuam vexāre. rēs adversās aequō
animō ferre dēbēmus. nōbīs crās reveniendum est.'   25

spē dēiectī *disappointed in their*
hope

philosopha *(female)*
philosopher
Athēnīs *at Athens*
odiō sunt: odiō esse *be hateful*
redeundum vōbīs est *you*
must return
nihilōminus *nevertheless*
perstitit: perstāre *persist*
arbiter *expert, judge*
ēlegantiae: ēlegantia *good*
taste
ergō *therefore*

dēpulit: dēpellere *push down*

mentem: mēns *mind*
aequō animō *calmly, with a*
calm mind

About the language 1: ablative absolute

1   Study the following pair of sentences:

mīlitēs discessērunt.
The soldiers departed.

urbe captā, mīlitēs discessērunt.
With the city having been captured, *the soldiers departed.*

The phrase in **bold type** is made up of a noun, **urbe**, and participle, **captā**, in the *ablative* case. Phrases of this kind are known as ablative absolute phrases, and are very common in Latin.

2   Ablative absolute phrases can be translated in many different ways. For instance, the example in paragraph 1 might be translated:

When the city had been captured, the soldiers departed.
Or,
After the city was captured, the soldiers departed.

3   Further examples:

a   arcū dēdicātō, cīvēs domum rediērunt.
b   pecūniā āmissā, ancilla lacrimāre coepit.
c   victimīs sacrificātīs, haruspex ōmina nūntiāvit.
d   duce interfectō, hostēs dēspērābant.
e   mercātor, clāmōribus audītīs, ē lectō perterritus surrēxit.
f   clientēs, iānuā clausā, invītī discessērunt.

4   In each of the examples above, the participle in the ablative absolute phrase is a perfect passive participle. Ablative absolute phrases can also be formed with present participles. For example:

omnibus tacentibus, lībertus nōmina recitāvit.
With everyone being quiet, *the freedman read out the names.*
Or, in more natural English:
When everyone was quiet, the freedman read out the names.

Further examples:

a   custōdibus dormientibus, captīvī effūgērunt.
b   pompā per viās prōcēdente, spectātōrēs vehementer plausērunt.
c   Imperātor, sacerdōtibus adstantibus, precēs dīvō Titō obtulit.

5 Ablative absolute phrases can also be formed with perfect active participles. For example:

> **dominō ēgressō**, servī garrīre coepērunt.
> ***With the master having gone out***, *the slaves began to chatter.*

Or, in more natural English:

> *After the master had gone out, the slaves began to chatter.*

Further examples:

a mercātōre profectō, rēs dīra accidit.
b nūntiīs ā Britanniā regressīs, imperātor senātōrēs arcessīvit.
c cōnsule haec locūtō, omnēs cīvēs attonitī erant.

Word patterns: compound verbs 2

1 Study the following verbs and their translations, and fill in the gaps in the table:

īre	abīre	circumīre	inīre
to go	*to go away*	*to go round*	....

dūcere	abdūcere	....	....
to lead	....	*to lead round*	*to lead in*

ferre	auferre (*originally* abferre)	circumferre	....
to carry, bring	*to carry away*	....	....

2 Give the meaning of the following compound verbs:

abicere	....	abesse	....	āvertere	....
circumstāre	....	circumvenīre	....	circumspectāre	....
īnfundere	....	immittere	....	irrumpere	....

3 Translate the following sentences, paying particular attention to the compound verbs:

a fabrī puellam circumvēnērunt, verba scurrīlia clāmantēs.
b cēnā parātā, servī vīnum in pōcula īnfūdērunt.
c clientēs, dēnāriīs raptīs, abiērunt ut cibum emerent.

4 The words in **bold type** in the following sentences are derived from Latin compound verbs. Explain the link between the Latin verbs and their English derivatives.

   a Salvius was hoping to **avert** the anger of Haterius.
   b Many philosophers are **circumspect** and consider all possibilities seriously.
   c An **induction** period is advisable in any new job.

Practising the language

1 Complete each sentence with the right form of the verb. Then translate the sentence. Note that the tense of the verb changes after sentence **c**.

   a ōlim multī leōnēs in Āfricā . . . . (captus est, captī sunt)
   b ecce! ille senex ā latrōnibus . . . . (vulnerātus est, vulnerātī sunt)
   c Haterius ā clientibus . . . . (salūtātus est, salūtātī sunt)
   d mīlitēs in ōrdinēs longōs ā centuriōnibus . . . . (īnstrūctus erat, īnstrūctī erant)
   e cīvēs spectāculō . . . . (dēlectātus erat, dēlectātī erant)
   f taurus ā sacerdōte . . . . (ēlēctus erat, ēlēctī erant)

2 Translate each sentence. Then change the words in **bold type** from singular to plural. Use the table of nouns on pp. 114–15 to help you.

   a mīles perfidus **amīcum** dēseruit.
   b dux virtūtem **legiōnis** laudāvit.
   c Imperātor multōs honōrēs **lībertō** dedit.
   d iūdex epistulam **testī** trādidit.
   e poēta librum **manū** tenuit.
   f puella, **flōre** dēlectāta, suāviter rīsit.
   g barbarī **vīllam agricolae** incendērunt.
   h rēx pecūniam **mātrī puerī** reddidit.

3 Complete each sentence with the most suitable word from the box below. Then translate the sentence.

   portābantur verbīs vītārent adeptī morbō abēgisset

   a puerī in fossam dēsiluērunt ut perīculum . . . .
   b Haterius, ... Salviī dēceptus, cōnsēnsit.
   c multae amphorae in triclīnium . . . .
   d senex, ... gravī afflīctus, medicum arcessīvit.
   e praecō, cum Euphrosynēn servumque . . . . , iānuam clausit.
   f clientēs, sportulam . . . . , abiērunt.

About the language 2: nē

1 In Stage 27, you met examples of indirect commands used with **ut**:

> imperāvit nūntiīs ut redīrent.
> *He ordered the messengers that they should return.*

Or, in more natural English:
> *He ordered the messengers to return.*

2 From Stage 29 onwards, you have met examples of indirect commands used with the word **nē**:

> imperāvit nūntiīs nē redīrent.
> *He ordered the messengers that they should not return.*

Or, in more natural English:
> *He ordered the messengers not to return.*

Further examples:

a haruspex iuvenem monuit nē nāvigāret.
b fēminae mīlitēs ōrāvērunt nē līberōs interficerent.
c mercātor amīcō persuāsit nē gemmās vēnderet.
d cūr vōbīs imperāvit nē vīllam intrārētis?

3 You have also met sentences in which **nē** is used with a purpose clause:

> senex pecūniam cēlāvit nē fūrēs eam invenīrent.
> *The old man hid the money lest the thieves should find it.*

Or, in more natural English:
> *The old man hid the money so that the thieves should not find it.*
> *The old man hid the money to prevent the thieves finding it.*

Further examples:

a per viās celeriter contendēbāmus nē ad arcum tardius advenīrēmus.
b in fossā latēbam nē hostēs mē cōnspicerent.
c imperātor multum frūmentum ab Aegyptō importāvit nē cīvēs famē perīrent.
d servī ē fundō effūgērunt nē poenās darent.

Rome's docklands.
Above: *A wharf with arched chambers for storing goods in transit.*
Below: *A Roman rubbish heap that still stands 30 metres high.*

The city of Rome

The city of Rome grew up in a very unplanned and unsystematic way, quite different from the neat grid-pattern of other Roman towns. It was also an extremely crowded city, with a population of approximately 1,000,000 people crammed into a small area.

The city was bounded on the western side by the river Tiber. Ships brought goods from the coastal port of Ostia and from the interior of Italy to the docks and riverside markets. Further upstream, beyond the wharves and warehouses, the river was divided for a short stretch by the Tiber Island (**Īnsula Tiberīna**). This elongated island, shown below and on p. 42, had been built up to look like a ship sailing the river, complete with an ornamental prow (**rōstrum**); it contained a temple of Aesculapius, the god of healing, to which many invalids came in hope of a cure.

Above: *The Tiber looking north, with the Island, centre, and Roman bridges.*
Left: *One of the Tiber riverboats, the* Isis Giminiana, *loading corn at Ostia to be taken to Rome. Her master, Farnaces, superintends the measuring of the corn from his place at the stern.*

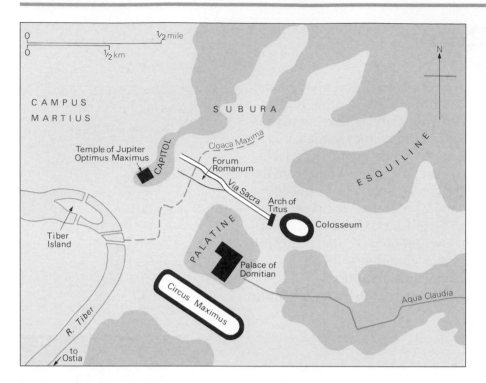

Central features of Rome
(1st century AD).

In the story on p. 42, Euphrosyne and her slave disembark near the Tiber Island and then move off north-eastwards. Their route could have taken them round the lower slopes of the Capitol and through the Forum Romanum (described in Stage 29), passing the Palatine hill where the Emperor Domitian had his palace.

Euphrosyne and the slave would then have continued through the Subura, a densely populated district north of the Forum, full of shops and large blocks of flats (īnsulae). Its inhabitants were mostly poor and some very poor indeed; they included barbers, shoemakers, butchers, weavers, blacksmiths, vegetable sellers, prostitutes and thieves. Several Roman writers refer to the Subura, and give a vivid impression of its noise, its dirt and its crowds. The following passage from Juvenal describes a street which might easily be in the Subura:

In the Subura, Euphrosyne would have passed stalls selling poultry, rabbits and vegetables (the monkeys were probably pets, not food). There were also blacksmiths' shops (below).

'We hurry on, but the way's blocked; there's a tidal wave of people in front, and we're pushed and prodded from behind. One man digs me with his elbow, another with the pole of a litter; somebody catches me on the head with a plank, and somebody else with a wine-barrel. My legs are plastered with mud, large feet trample on me from every side, and a soldier is sticking the nail of his boot in my toe.'

Many rich and aristocratic Romans settled in the district of the Esquiline hill, which lay to the east of the Subura. Here they could enjoy peace and seclusion in huge mansions, surrounded by colonnaded gardens and landscaped parks which contrasted very sharply with the Subura's slums and crowded tenement blocks. In the stories of Book IV, Haterius' house, where Euphrosyne's journey ended, is imagined as being on the Esquiline.

Two views of a prestigious shopping development in Rome, built by the Emperor Trajan. Most of the Subura streets were much more ramshackle.

In the large picture, we are inside a shop, looking across the street towards two more. The one opposite has a window above the shop doorway to light the shop after the shutters were closed; the shopkeeper would probably live there. Above that is the arched support for a balcony belonging to the flat above – the block is several storeys high.

In the shop on this side we can see the groove to hold the shutters, and also two square holes (left) for the bars that held the shutters in place.

Among the well-known landmarks of Rome were the Circus Maximus (south of the Palatine), where chariot-races were held, the Colosseum (see p. 37), which lay between the Esquiline and the eastern end of the Sacred Way, and the Campus Martius on the western side of the city, formerly an army training area and place for assemblies. It still provided some much needed open space for the general population, but was increasingly built upon in the time of the emperors.

People's palaces

Left: *The interior of the Colosseum. The animal cages and machinery below were originally hidden by a wooden floor spread with sand.*

Below: *The Circus Maximus, with Domitian's palace on the Palatine overlooking it on the left. You can see the central 'spine' of the circus round which the chariots raced – it has a tree planted at the nearer end.*

Above: *Here and there in modern Rome, remains of the ancient aqueduct system can still be seen, dwarfing the houses. Compare the aqueduct on the right-hand side of the picture on p. 1.*
Left: *An aqueduct approaching Rome. It carried two water channels, one above the other.*

Crossing the city in various directions were the aqueducts, which brought water into the city at the rate of 900 million litres a day. The houses of the rich citizens were usually connected to this supply by means of pipes which brought water directly into their storage tanks; the poorer people had to collect their fresh water from public fountains on street corners. The city also possessed a very advanced system of drains and sewers: a complicated network of underground channels carried sewage and waste water from the larger private houses, public baths, fountains and lavatories to the central drain (**Cloāca Maxima**), which emptied into the Tiber.

There were many hazards and discomforts for the inhabitants of Rome. As we have seen in Stage 30 (p. 36), fires were frequent and the insulae in the slums were often badly built and liable to collapse. The overcrowding and congestion in the streets have already been mentioned above; wheeled traffic was banned from the city centre during the hours of daylight, but blockages were still caused by the wagons of builders like Haterius, which were exempt from the ban. Disease was an ever-present danger in the overcrowded poorer quarters; crime and violence were commonplace in the unlit streets at night. Rome was a city of contrasts, in which splendour and squalor were often found side by side; it could be both an exciting and an unpleasant place to live.

Patronage

The story on pp. 44–6 shows an aspect of Roman society known as patronage, in which a patron (**patrōnus**) gave help and protection to others less rich or powerful than himself, and they performed various services for him in return.

There were many different types of patronage: for example, the emperor regularly nominated a senator to be one of the next year's consuls; a rich businessman would introduce a merchant to some useful contacts; a poet's patron would arrange for the poet to recite his work to an audience, or provide him with money or presents, sometimes on a very generous scale. In each case, the patron would expect not only gratitude but service in return. A poet, for example, would praise the patron in his poetry; the Romans would regard this not as sickly flattery, but as a normal and proper thing to do.

The letters written by Pliny often give us glimpses of patronage in operation. Once, when Pliny was asked to speak in a case in court, he agreed on condition that a young friend of his, who had plenty of ability but had not yet had any chance to show how good he was, should be allowed to make a speech too. And when Pliny's friend Erucius stood as an election candidate, Pliny wrote to an influential ex-consul (and no doubt to other people too), asking him to support Erucius and persuade others to do the same. Pliny was also patron of his home town Comum in north Italy, and of the little town of Tifernum-on-Tiber. He gave generous gifts of buildings and money to both places.

But the commonest type of patronage was the type illustrated on pp. 44–6, in which the patron looked after a number of poorer people who depended on him for support or employment. They were known as clients (**clientēs**). A client was expected to present himself at his patron's house each day for the **salūtātiō** or early morning ceremony of greeting, at which he hoped to receive a gift known as the **sportula**. In the past, the sportula had consisted of a little basket of food, but by Domitian's time it was normally money; the standard amount was fixed by custom at 6.25 sesterces. A client was expected to dress formally in a toga for the salutatio. He also had to address his patron as **domine**; the poet Martial complains that when he once forgot to do this, the patron punished him by giving him no sportula.

In addition to the sportula, the client might receive help of other kinds from his patron. His patron might advise him if he was in trouble, give him occasional presents, perhaps find him employment or speak on his behalf in court. Occasionally clients might be invited to dinner at their patron's house. At these dinners, as we know from the angry comments of several Roman writers, some patrons served two different qualities of

Just as Pliny was patron of his home town, so Holconius Rufus was patron of Pompeii.

food and wine: a superior quality for themselves and their close friends, and a poor one for the clients. Some patrons did this to save money, others to make it clear that they regarded their clients as inferiors.

In return for this help a patron would expect his clients not only to attend the salutatio, but also to perform various tasks and errands for him. For example, he might require some of them to escort him when he went to the Forum on official business, or to witness the signing of a legal document, or to lead the applause if he made a public speech in court or elsewhere, or to help him at election time. It seems likely that for many clients their duties were not difficult but could be very boring and time-consuming.

Both patrons and clients had something to gain from the system. The government did not provide any state assistance, apart from distributions of free grain or occasionally money to a limited number of citizens, and so a patron might be a client's chief means of support. The main advantage for the patron was that he was able to call on the services of his clients when he needed them; and to have a large number of clients was good for his prestige and status.

One special type of patron-client relationship (which we shall see more of in Stage 34) should be mentioned: the relationship between ex-master and his former slave. When a slave was set free, he automatically became a client of his ex-master, and his ex-master became his patron. The word **patrōnus** is sometimes used with the meaning 'ex-master' as well as the meaning 'patron'.

One man could be the patron of another who in turn was the patron of somebody else. The diagram on the right shows how several people could be linked by patronage.

The emperor had no patron. He was the most powerful patron of all.

EMPEROR nominates SALVIUS to an important priesthood

SALVIUS obtains building contract for HATERIUS

HATERIUS orders distribution of sportula to CLIENTS

The patronage system.

Vocabulary checklist 31

altus, alta, altum	high, deep
ante	before, in front of
cōnsistō, cōnsistere, cōnstitī	halt, stand one's ground
dux, ducis	leader
frūmentum, frūmentī	grain
haudquāquam	not at all
īdem, eadem, idem	the same
identidem	repeatedly
nē	that not, so that … not
neglegō, neglegere, neglēxī, neglēctus	neglect, ignore, disregard
ōrō, ōrāre, ōrāvī	beg
prōgressus, prōgressa, prōgressum	having advanced
rapiō, rapere, rapuī, raptus	seize, grab
scindō, scindere, scidī, scissus	tear, tear up
spērō, spērāre, spērāvī	hope, expect
superbus, superba, superbum	arrogant, proud
tempus, temporis	time
undique	on all sides, from all sides
vehō, vehere, vexī, vectus	carry
vinciō, vincīre, vīnxī, vīnctus	bind, tie up
volvō, volvere, volvī, volūtus	turn, roll
vultus, vultūs	expression, face

This large stone disc is the Bocca della Verità, or Mouth of Truth. It is said that if you put your hand in the mouth and tell a lie, the mouth will close and crush your hand. But originally it was a Roman sewer cover, probably from the Cloaca Maxima.

EUPHROSYNE

STAGE 32

1 postrīdiē Euphrosynē domum Hateriī
regressa est. iterum tamen praecō eam verbīs
dūrīs abēgit.

regressa est *returned*

2 servus eam hortātus est ut praecōnem dōnīs
corrumperet; sed Euphrosynē ab eiusmodī
ambitiōne abhorruit.

hortātus est *urged*
dōnīs corrumperet: dōnīs corrumpere *bribe*
eiusmodī *of that kind*
ambitiōne: ambitiō *bribery, corruption*

3 Euphrosynē, septem continuōs diēs ā praecōne
abācta, dēnique in Graeciam redīre cōnstituit.
hōc cōnsiliō captō, ad flūmen Tiberim ut nāvem
cōnscenderet profecta est.

abācta: abigere *drive away*
profecta est *set out*

4 eōdem diē quō Euphrosynē discēdere cōnstituit,
celebrābat Haterius diem nātālem.
grātulātiōnibus clientium acceptīs, ōtiōsus in
hortō sedēbat. subitō Eryllus hortum ingressus
est.

ingressus est *entered*

Euphrosynē revocāta

revocāta: revocāre *recall, call back*

I

Eryllus, cum hortum intrāvisset, Haterium verbīs blandīs adlocūtus est.

adlocūtus est *addressed, spoke to*

Eryllus:	domine! omnia quae mandāvistī parāta sunt. centum amīcī et clientēs ad cēnam invītātī sunt. iussī coquum cibum sūmptuōsum parāre, cellāriumque 5 vīnum Falernum veterrimum praebēre. nihil neglēctum est.
Haterius:	nōnne petauristāriōs vel saltātrīcēs condūxistī? hercle! quam mē dēlectant petauristāriī!
Eryllus:	quid dīcis, domine? hominēs eiusmodī cīvibus 10 urbānīs nōn placent. nunc philosophīs favet optimus quisque.
Haterius:	īnsānīs, Erylle! nam philosophī sunt senēs sevērī. nec saltāre nec circulōs trānsilīre possunt.
Eryllus:	at domine, aliquid melius quam philosophum 15 adeptus sum. mē enim auctōre, philosopha quaedam, puella pulcherrima, hūc invītāta est. ā Chrȳsogonō Athēnīs missa est.
Haterius:	philosopham mīsit Chrȳsogonus? optimē fēcistī, Erylle! philosopham nē Imperātor quidem habet. sed 20 ubi est haec philosopha quam adeptus es?
Eryllus:	iamdūdum eam anxius exspectō. fortasse iste praecō, homō summae stultitiae, eam nōn admīsit.
Haterius:	arcesse hūc praecōnem!

vīnum Falernum *Falernian wine (a very expensive wine)*
veterrimum: vetus *old*
petauristāriōs: petauristārius *acrobat*
vel *or*
optimus quisque *all the best people (literally each excellent person)*
sevērī: sevērus *severe, strict*
nec ... nec *neither ... nor*
circulōs: circulus *hoop*
trānsilīre *jump through*
at *but*
adeptus sum *I have obtained*
mē ... auctōre *at my suggestion*
quaedam: quīdam *a certain*
iamdūdum *for a long time*

II

ubi praecō ingressus est, Haterius rogāvit utrum philosopham abēgisset necne. poenās maximās eī minātus est. praecō, verbīs dominī perterritus, palluit; tōtā rē nārrātā, veniam ōrāvit.

utrum ... necne *whether ... or not*
minātus est *threatened*

praecō:	domine, ignōsce mihi! nesciēbam quantum tū philosophīs favērēs. illa philosopha, quam ignārus 5 abēgī, ad flūmen profecta est ut nāvem cōnscenderet.
Haterius:	abī statim, caudex! festīnā ad Tiberim! nōlī umquam revenīre nisi cum philosophā!

ignōsce: ignōscere *forgive*

domō ēgressus, praecō per viās contendit. ad flūmen cum advēnisset, 10 Euphrosynēn in nāvem cōnscēnsūram cōnspexit. magnā vōce eam appellāvit. Euphrosynē, nōmine audītō, cōnstitit.

Euphrosynēn *Greek accusative of* Euphrosynē
cōnscēnsūram: cōnscēnsūrus *about to go on board*

praecō:	ignōsce mihi, Euphrosynē doctissima! nōlī discēdere! necesse est tibi domum Hateriī mēcum prōcēdere.
Euphrosynē:	cūr mē revocās? odiō sunt omnēs philosophī Hateriō, ut tū ipse dīxistī. Athēnās igitur nunc redeō. valē!

15

deinde praecō, effūsīs lacrimīs, eam identidem ōrāvit nē discēderet.
diū Euphrosynē perstitit; dēnique, precibus lacrimīsque eius 20
commōta, domum Haterii regressa est.

effūsīs lacrimīs *with tears pouring out, bursting into tears*

cēna Haterii

nōnā hōrā amīcī clientēsque, quōs Haterius invītāverat ut sēcum
diem nātālem celebrārent, triclīnium ingrediēbantur. inter eōs
aderant fīliī lībertōrum quī humilī locō nātī magnās opēs adeptī
erant. aderant quoque nōnnūllī senātōrēs quī inopiā oppressī
favōrem Haterii petēbant. 5
    proximus Hateriō recumbēbat T. Flāvius Sabīnus cōnsul, vir
summae auctōritātis. spē favōris, Haterius Sabīnum blandīs et
mollibus verbīs adloquēbātur. ipse ānulōs gerēbat aureōs quī
gemmīs fulgēbant; dentēs spīnā argenteā perfodiēbat.
    intereā duo Aethiopes triclīnium ingrediēbantur. lancem 10
ingentem ferēbant, in quā positus erat aper tōtus. statim coquus,
quī Aethiopas in triclīnium secūtus erat, ad lancem prōgressus
est ut aprum secāret. aprō perītē sectō, multae avēs statim
ēvolāvērunt, suāviter pīpiantēs. hospitēs, cum vīdissent quid
coquus parāvisset, eius artem vehementer laudāvērunt. quā rē 15
dēlectātus, Haterius servīs imperāvit ut amphorās vīnī Falernī
īnferrent. amphorīs inlātīs, cellārius titulōs quī īnfīxī erant

ingrediēbantur *were entering*

inopiā: inopia *poverty*
proximus *next to*
adloquēbātur *was addressing*
dentēs: dēns *tooth*
spīnā: spīna *toothpick*
perfodiēbat: perfodere *pick*
lancem: lānx *dish*
aper *boar*
secāret: secāre *carve*
avēs: avis *bird*
pīpiantēs: pīpiāre *chirp*
titulōs: titulus *label*
īnfīxī erant: īnfīgere *fasten onto*

magnā vōce recitāvit, 'Falernum Hateriānum, vīnum centum annōrum!' tum vīnum in pōcula servī īnfundere coepērunt.

hospitibus laetissimē bibentibus, poposcit Haterius silentium. *20* rīdēns digitīs concrepuit. signō datō appāruērunt in līmine duo tubicinēs. tubās vehementer īnflāvērunt. tum Eryllus Euphrosynēn in triclīnium dūxit. hospitēs, simulatque eam vīdērunt, fōrmam eius valdē admīrātī sunt.

Haterius rīdēns Euphrosynēn rogāvit ut sēcum in lectō *25* cōnsīderet. deinde hospitēs adlocūtus est.

'haec puella', inquit glōriāns, 'est philosopha doctissima, nōmine Euphrosynē. iussū meō hūc vēnit Athēnīs, ubi habitant philosophī nōtissimī. illa nōbīs dīligenter audienda est.'

tum ad eam conversus, *30*

'nōbīs placet, mea Euphrosynē', inquit, 'ā tē aliquid philosophiae discere.'

Hateriānum: Hateriānus *belonging to Haterius*
īnfundere *pour into*
digitīs: digitus *finger*
concrepuit: concrepāre *snap, click*
fōrmam: fōrma *beauty, appearance*
admīrātī sunt *admired*
glōriāns *boasting, boastfully*

About the language 1: deponent verbs

1 Study the following examples:

> clientēs pecūniam rapere **cōnābantur**.
> *The clients **were trying** to grab the money.*

> praecō tandem **locūtus est**.
> *At last the herald **spoke**.*

Notice the form and meaning of the words in **bold type**. Each verb has a *passive ending* (**-bantur, -tus est**) but an *active meaning (they were trying, he spoke)*. Verbs of this kind are known as deponent verbs.

2 Study the following forms of two common deponent verbs:

present

cōnātur	s/he tries	loquitur	s/he speaks
cōnantur	they try	loquuntur	they speak

imperfect

cōnābātur	s/he was trying	loquēbātur	s/he was speaking
cōnābantur	they were trying	loquēbantur	they were speaking

perfect

cōnātus est	he (has) tried	locūtus est	he spoke, he has spoken
cōnātī sunt	they (have) tried	locūtī sunt	they spoke, they have spoken

pluperfect

cōnātus erat	he had tried	locūtus erat	he had spoken
cōnātī erant	they had tried	locūtī erant	they had spoken

3 Further examples:

    a spectātōrēs dē arcū novō loquēbantur.
    b captīvus effugere cōnātus est.
    c sacerdōs ē templō ēgrediēbātur.
    d fabrī puellam cōnspicātī sunt.
    e sequēbantur; ingressus est; precātur; regrediuntur; profectī erant; suspicātus erat.

4 You have already met the perfect participles of several deponent verbs. For example:

    adeptus   *having obtained*
    hortātus   *having encouraged*
    regressus   *having returned*

Compare them with the perfect participles of some ordinary verbs (i.e. verbs which are not deponent):

deponent		*ordinary*	
adeptus	*having obtained*	dēceptus	*having been deceived*
hortātus	*having encouraged*	laudātus	*having been praised*
regressus	*having returned*	missus	*having been sent*

Notice that:
    the deponent perfect participle has an *active* meaning;
    the ordinary perfect participle has a *passive* meaning.

5 Give the meanings of the following perfect participles from deponent and ordinary verbs.

deponent	*ordinary*
cōnspicātus	portātus
ingressus	iussus
profectus	afflīctus
locūtus	audītus
cōnātus	vulnerātus

A model of rich people's houses in their parks and gardens. Haterius would have lived in a similar mansion.

philosophia

philosophia *philosophy*

Euphrosynē hospitēs, quī avidē spectābant, sīc adlocūta est:
   'prīmum, fābula brevis mihi nārranda est. ōlim fuit homō
pauper quī fundum parvum, uxōrem optimam, līberōs
cārissimōs habēbat. strēnuē in fundō labōrāre solēbat ut sibi
suīsque cibum praebēret.'

   'scīlicet īnsānus erat', exclāmāvit Apollōnius, quī erat homō
ignāvissimus. 'nēmō nisi īnsānus labōrat.'

   cui respondit Euphrosynē vōce serēnā,

   'omnibus autem labōrandum est. etiam eī quī spē favōris
cēnās magistrātibus dant, rē vērā labōrant.'

   quō audītō, Haterius ērubuit; cēterī, verbīs Euphrosynēs
obstupefactī, tacēbant. deinde Euphrosynē

   'pauper', inquit, 'nec nimium edēbat nec nimium bibēbat. in
omnibus vītae partibus temperāns esse cōnābātur.'

   L. Baebius Crispus senātor exclāmāvit,

   'scīlicet avārus erat! ille pauper nōn laudandus est nōbīs sed
culpandus. Haterius noster tamen maximē laudandus est quod
amīcīs sūmptuōsās cēnās semper praebet.'

   huic Baebiī sententiae omnēs plausērunt. Haterius, plausū
audītō, oblītus philosophiae servīs imperāvit ut plūs vīnī
hospitibus offerrent. Euphrosynē tamen haec addidit:

   'at pauper multōs cāsūs passus est. uxōrem enim et līberōs
āmīsit, morbō gravissimō afflīctōs; fundum āmīsit, ā
mīlitibus dīreptum; postrēmō ipse, inopiā oppressus et in
servitūtem abductus, lībertātem āmīsit. nihilōminus, quia
Stōicus erat, rēs adversās semper aequō animō patiēbātur.
tandem senectūte labōribusque cōnfectus, tranquillē mortuus
est. ille pauper, quem hominēs miserrimum exīstimābant, rē
vērā fēlīx erat.'

   Haterius attonitus 'num fēlīcem eum exīstimās', inquit, 'quī
tot cāsūs passus est?'

   sed priusquam Euphrosynē eī respondēret, cōnsul
Sabīnus

   'satis philosophiae!' inquit. 'age, mea Euphrosynē, dā mihi
ōsculum, immo ōscula multa.'

   Rabīrius Maximus tamen, quī cum haec audīvisset ēbrius
surrēxit,

   'sceleste', inquit, 'nōlī eam tangere!'

   haec locūtus, pōculum vīnō plēnum in ōs Sabīnī iniēcit.

   statim rēs ad pugnam vēnit. pōcula iaciēbantur; mensae
ēvertēbantur; togae scindēbantur. aliī Sabīnō, aliī Rabīriō
subveniēbant. Haterius hūc illūc currēbat; discordiam
compōnere frūstrā cōnābātur.

   Euphrosynē autem, ad iānuam triclīniī vultū serēnō
prōgressa, hospitēs pugnantēs ita adlocūta est:

5   **suīs: suī** *his family*
scīlicet *obviously*

10   **rē vērā** *in fact, truly*
Euphrosynēs *Greek genitive of*
   Euphrosynē
edēbat: edere *eat*
temperāns *temperate, self-
   controlled*

15

culpandus: culpāre *blame*

plausū: plausus *applause*
20   **oblītus** *having forgotten*

cāsūs: cāsus *misfortune*

25   **abductus: abdūcere** *lead away*
Stōicus *Stoic (believer in Stoic
   philosophy)*
patiēbātur *suffered, endured*
senectūte: senectūs *old age*
30   **tranquillē** *peacefully*
exīstimābant: exīstimāre
   think, consider
priusquam *before*
immo *or rather*

35

40

discordiam, discordia *strife*
compōnere *settle*

45

'ēn Rōmānī, dominī orbis terrārum, ventris Venerisque servī!'
quibus verbīs dictīs, ad flūmen Tiberim ut nāvem quaereret
profecta est.

orbis terrārum *world*
Veneris: Venus *Venus*
(goddess of love)

Questions for discussion

1 Why was Euphrosyne's philosophy lecture a failure?
2 Look again at Euphrosyne's remark **'ille pauper … rē vērā fēlīx erat'** (lines 28–29). Was Haterius right to suggest that this is a stupid remark? Or does it have some point?
3 **ēn Rōmānī … servī** (line 46). What experiences at Haterius' dinner party led Euphrosyne to make this comment?

About the language 2: more about gerundives

1 In Stage 26, you met the gerundive used in sentences like this:

mihi currendum est.
I must run.

2 In Stage 32, you have met more sentences containing gerundives. For example:

mihi fābula nārranda est.
I must tell a story.

Compare this with another way of expressing the same idea:

necesse est mihi fābulam nārrāre.

3 Further examples:

a mihi epistula scrībenda est.
b tibi testāmentum faciendum est.
c nōbīs Haterius vīsitandus est.
d coquō cēna paranda est.
e mihi dignitās servanda est.
f tibi puella in vīllam admittenda est.

Word patterns: verbs and nouns

1 As you have already seen in Stage 26, some verbs and nouns are closely connected. Here are further examples:

verb		fourth declension noun	
lūgēre	*to lament*	lūctus	*grief*
metuere	*to fear*	metus	*fear*
currere	*to run*	cursus	*track, course*

Put the following words into four verb and noun pairs. Then translate them.

plausus, sonitus, cōnspicere, cantus, sonāre, cantāre, cōnspectus, plaudere.

2 The following nouns are connected with verbs you already know. Match them with the correct English translation.

Latin: exitus, monitus, cōnsēnsus, reditus
English: *return, way out, agreement, warning.*

3 From the box choose the correct Latin words to translate the words in **bold type** in the following sentences:

rīsus   rīdēre   mōtus   adventus   advenīre   movēre

a The **motion** of the crane made Salvius feel sick.
b Haterius tried not **to smile**.
c The **arrival** of the emperor was eagerly awaited.

Practising the language

1 Complete each sentence by describing the word in **bold type** with the correct form of the adjective in brackets. Use paragraphs 1 and 2 on p. 116 to help you. Then translate the sentence.

For example: clientēs **patrōnum** . . . . laudāvērunt. (līberālis)
Answer: clientēs patrōnum līberālem laudāvērunt.
               The clients praised their generous patron.

The gender of some of the words in **bold type** is given after the word.

a nautae **nāvem** (f.) . . . . comparāvērunt. (optimus)
b coquus īram **dominī** . . . . timēbat. (crūdēlis)
c mercātor, **itinere** (n.) . . . . fessus, in rīpā flūminis cōnsēdit. (longus)
d senex testāmentum **amīcō** . . . . mandāvit. (fidēlis)
e centuriō verba **uxōris** . . . . neglēxit. (īrātus)
f **saxa** (n.) . . . . ad arcum ā fabrīs trahēbantur. (gravis)
g subitō vōcēs **mīlitum** . . . . audīvimus. (noster)
h Euphrosynē **hospitibus** . . . . statim respondit. (īnsolēns)

2   In each pair of sentences, translate the first sentence; then change it from a direct command to an indirect command by completing the second sentence with an imperfect subjunctive. Then translate the second sentence.

For example: pontem incende!
               centuriō mīlitī imperāvit ut pontem incender... .

Translated and completed, this becomes:

            pontem incende!
            Burn the bridge down!

            centuriō mīlitī imperāvit ut pontem incenderet.
            The centurion ordered the soldier to burn the bridge down.

The forms of the imperfect subjunctive are given on p. 128.

a   pecūniam cēlāte!
        mercātor amīcōs monuit ut pecūniam cēlār... .
b   arcum mihi ostende!
        puer patrem ōrāvit ut arcum sibi ostender... .
c   iānuam aperīte!
        imperātor nōbīs imperāvit ut iānuam aperīr... .
d   nōlīte redīre!
        nūntius barbarīs persuāsit nē redīr... .

In sentences **e** and **f**, turn the direct command into an indirect command by adding the necessary words to the second sentence:

e   cēnam optimam parāte!
        dominus servīs imperāvit ut . . . .
f   epistulam scrībe!
        frāter mihi persuāsit . . . .

About the language 3: future participles

1 Study the following examples:

> nunc ego quoque **moritūrus** sum.
> *Now I, too, am about to die.*

> nēmō sciēbat quid Haterius **factūrus** esset.
> *Nobody knew what Haterius was going to do.*

> praecō puellam vīdit, nāvem **cōnscēnsūram**.
> *The herald saw the girl about to go on board ship.*

The words in **bold type** are future participles.

2 Further examples:

   a nunc ego vōbīs cēnam splendidam datūrus sum.
   b mīlitēs in animō volvēbant quid centuriō dictūrus esset.
   c hospitēs Haterium rogāvērunt num Euphrosynē saltātūra esset.
   d custōdēs fūrēs cēpērunt, pecūniam ablātūrōs.

3 Compare the future participle with the perfect passive participle:

perfect passive participle	*future participle*
portātus	portātūrus
having been carried	*about to carry*
doctus	doctūrus
having been taught	*about to teach*
tractus	tractūrus
having been dragged	*about to drag*
audītus	audītūrus
having been heard	*about to hear*

Roman society

This diagram shows one way of dividing up Roman society:

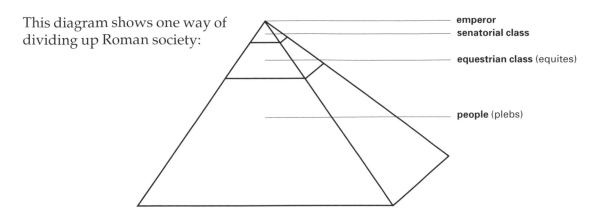

- **emperor**
- **senatorial class**
- **equestrian class** (equites)
- **people** (plebs)

senātōrēs

At the top of the pyramid is the emperor. Below him are the men of the senatorial class or **senātōrēs**. Membership of this group was generally by inheritance (in other words, members' sons were automatically qualified to become members themselves); membership could also be given to an individual by the emperor as a special privilege. A man who was in the senatorial class had the opportunity to follow a political career which could lead (if he were good enough or had influence with the emperor) to high positions such as the command of a legion, the consulship, or the governorship of a province. Both Agricola and Salvius are examples of men who reached high positions of this kind.

Members of the senatorial class also possessed various privileges to emphasise their status: they wore a broad purple stripe on their tunics, sat in special places reserved for them at public ceremonies and entertainments, and were eligible for special honours such as certain priesthoods. To retain their membership, however, men of the senatorial class had to possess 1,000,000 sesterces in money or property. Occasionally a senatorial family's wealth dropped below the 1,000,000-sesterce line. When this happened, the members of the family, like the senators at the party on p. 63, were in danger of being expelled from the senatorial class by the 'censors', who had the job of periodically bringing the membership list up to date.

The Curia or senate house in the Forum Romanum.

equitēs

Below the senatorial class are the men of the wealthy equestrian class or **equitēs**. They were called equites because, according to legend, wealthy citizens had been recruited by the early kings of

Rome to form the cavalry in the army. The qualification for membership of this class was 400,000 sesterces. The equites could follow a career in government if they wished, at a rather humbler level than the senatorial career; they might, for example, command an auxiliary unit in the army or supervise a province's financial affairs. If they were exceptionally able or lucky, they might rise to the highest positions in an equestrian career, such as the command of the praetorian guard or the governorship of Egypt. Signs of equestrian status included the wearing of a special gold ring, and a narrow stripe on the tunic. A number of equites, like Haterius in the stories in Book IV, were extremely rich – richer in fact than many senators. Some were offered promotion by the emperor into the senatorial class, though not all of them chose to accept.

plēbs

Below the equites are the ordinary citizens, or **plēbs**. As the diagram indicates, they formed the great mass of the Roman population. Some of them earned a reasonably comfortable living as craftsmen or shopkeepers, or ran small businesses. Many depended on casual and irregular employment (as porters, for example, or as temporary labourers on building sites). Others lived in poverty, surviving with the help of their patron or, if they were resident in Rome, on the public distribution of free grain made by the emperor's officials to some citizens. In general, the plebs were entirely excluded from positions of power and prestige. A few, however, through hard work or luck or their patron's assistance, succeeded in becoming equites or even (very rarely) reaching the senatorial class.

Much free grain was distributed to the poor. Here a consignment of grain is being measured.

Astrology, philosophy and other beliefs

Many Romans were content with the official state religion and its rituals of prayer, divination and sacrifice, described in Stage 23. Some, however, found greater satisfaction in other forms of belief, including astrology, philosophy and foreign cults. Many took part in both the state religion and some other kind of worship, without feeling that there was any conflict between the two.

Astrology

One popular form of belief, which you met in Book II, was astrology. Astrologers claimed that the events in a person's life were controlled by the stars, and that it was possible to forecast the future by studying the positions and movements of stars and planets. The position of the stars at the time of a person's birth was known as a horoscope and regarded as particularly important. Astrology was officially disapproved of, especially if people used it to try to find out when their relatives or acquaintances were going to die, and from time to time all astrologers were banished from Rome. (They were always back again within a few months.) In particular, it was a serious offence to enquire about the horoscope of the emperor. Several emperors, however, were themselves firm believers in astrology and kept private astrologers of their own.

A diagram of the heavens, from a villa at Stabiae, near Pompeii.

Stoicism

A few Romans, especially those who had come into contact with Greek ideas through education or travel, became interested in philosophy. Philosophy was concerned with such questions as: 'What is the world made of?' 'What happens to us after we die?' 'What is the right way to live?' In particular, a number of Romans were attracted by the philosophy of Stoicism. Stoics believed, like Euphrosyne in the story on pp. 66–7, that the aim in life should be Virtue (right behaviour) rather than Pleasure;

that a clear conscience, self-reliance and doing one's duty brought deeper satisfaction than material possessions and self-indulgence. The philosopher Seneca, who taught the Emperor Nero, wrote:

> 'Virtue is found in temples, in the forum and the senate-house, defending the city walls, covered in dust, burnt by the sun, with hands hardened by toil; Pleasure is found skulking in the shadows, lurking in baths and brothels and places which fear the police, soft, flabby and gutless, soaked in scent and wine, with a face pale or painted with cosmetics.'

At the time of the stories in Stage 32, the most important Stoic philosopher in Rome was a Greek named Epictetus. Epictetus had formerly been a slave; the lameness from which he suffered was said to have been caused by brutal treatment at the hands of his master (the Emperor's freedman, Epaphroditus). While still a slave, Epictetus was allowed to attend philosophy lectures, and when he was freed he became a philosophy teacher himself and attracted large audiences.

Stoics tended to disapprove of one-man rule, and to prefer the idea of a republic. They did not think supreme political power should be passed on by inheritance from one ruler to the next, and they thought a ruler should aim to benefit all his subjects, not just a few. As a result of this, at various times during the first century, a number of Roman Stoics challenged the power of the emperor, opposed him in the Senate, or even plotted to kill him. Their efforts were unsuccessful, and they were punished by exile or death.

Euphrosyne is fictional. Most philosophers were male, as Haterius said in the story. Their portraits show rather forbidding characters, like Chrysippos, one of the early Stoics, below.

Mithraism

Some Romans became followers of foreign cults, especially those that involved dramatic initiation ceremonies or offered hope of life after death. One such cult was the religion of Isis, whose ritual was described in Stage 19. Another was Mithraism, or Mithras-worship. Mithras was a god of light and truth, who triumphed over the forces of evil, and promised life after death to his followers. His powers were summed up in the story of his chief exploit: the capture and killing of a mighty bull, whose blood had the power to give new life. There were seven grades of initiation into Mithraism, each with its own secret ceremony, involving tests and ordeals of various kinds. Lying in a pit formed part of one ceremony; branding may have formed part of another.

Mithraism expected high standards of conduct from its followers; it laid great stress on courage and loyalty, and became popular in the army. Nevertheless, it was a rather expensive and exclusive religion; those who were initiated seem to have been mainly army officers (rather than ordinary legionaries) or wealthy businessmen. A number of Mithraic temples have been discovered, including one in London and another at Carrawburgh in Northumberland, close to Hadrian's Wall.

Isis-worship and Mithraism both came to Rome from the east, Isis-worship from Egypt and Mithraism from Persia. From the east, too, came Christianity, which was at first disliked by the Romans and at times was fiercely attacked, but eventually became the official religion of the Roman empire. It will be described more fully in Stage 33.

Mithraea

Temples of Mithras were constructed to look like caves; the one on the left is in Rome. Banqueting couches line the two sides and there is a relief showing the god slaying the bull. Below is an artist's reconstruction of a ceremony in progress.

Vocabulary checklist 32

adversus, adversa, adversum	*hostile, unfavourable*
rēs adversae	*misfortune*
aequus, aequa, aequum	*fair, calm*
compōnō, compōnere, composuī,	
compositus	*put together, arrange, settle*
cōnātus, cōnāta, cōnātum	*having tried*
convertō, convertere, convertī,	
conversus	*turn*
effundō, effundere, effūdī,	
effūsus	*pour out*
ignōscō, ignōscere, ignōvī	*forgive*
labor, labōris	*work, labour*
lībertās, lībertātis	*freedom*
mēnsa, mēnsae	*table*
nē … quidem	*not even*
nec	*and not, nor*
nec … nec	*neither … nor*
opprimō, opprimere, oppressī,	
oppressus	*crush*
ōtiōsus, ōtiōsa, ōtiōsum	*idle, on holiday*
pauper, *gen.* **pauperis**	*poor*
profectus, profecta, profectum	*having set out*
quīdam, quaedam, quoddam	*one, a certain*
secūtus, secūta, secūtum	*having followed*
subveniō, subvenīre, subvēnī	*help, come to help*

Mithras slaying the bull, framed by the zodiac symbols. A relief from Roman London.

PANTOMIMUS

STAGE 33

1 praecō prīmus: fābula! fābula optima!
                         Paris, pantomīmus nōtissimus, in theātrō crās fābulam aget.
                         Myropnous, tībīcen perītissimus, tībiīs cantābit.

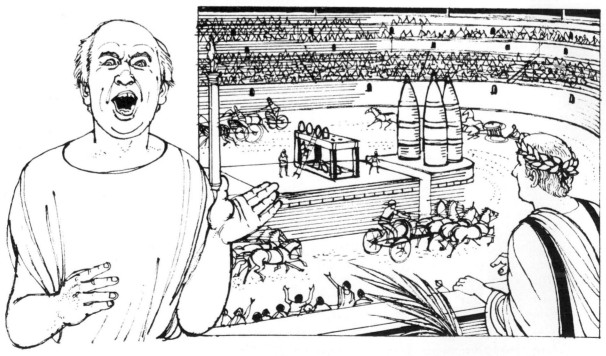

2 praecō secundus: lūdī! lūdī magnificī!
                          duodecim aurīgae in Circō Maximō crās certābunt.
                          Imperātor ipse victōrī praemium dabit.

3 praecō tertius: spectāculum! spectāculum splendidum!
quīnquāgintā gladiātōrēs in amphitheātrō Flāviō crās pugnābunt.
multus sanguis fluet.

Tychicus

in hortō Hateriī fābula agēbātur. Paris, pantomīmus nōtissimus,
mortem rēgīnae Dīdōnis imitābātur. aderant multī spectātōrēs
quī ā Vitelliā, uxōre Hateriī, invītātī erant.

    Paris mōtibus ēlegantissimīs aptissimīsque dolōrem rēgīnae
morientis imitābātur. cum dēnique quasi mortuus prōcubuisset,   5
omnēs spectātōrēs admīrātiōne affectī identidem plaudēbant.
aliī flōrēs iactābant, aliī Paridem deum appellābant. surrēxit
Paris ut plausum spectātōrum exciperet.

    sed priusquam ille plūra ageret, vir quīdam statūrā brevī
vultūque sevērō prōgressus magnā vōce silentium poposcit.   10
oculīs in eum statim conversīs, spectātōrēs quis esset et quid
vellet rogābant. paucī eum agnōvērunt. Iūdaeus erat, Tychicus
nōmine, cliēns T. Flāviī Clēmentis. Paris ipse fābulā interruptā
adeō obstupefactus est ut stāret immōtus. omnīnō ignōrābat
quid Tychicus factūrus esset.   15

pantomīmus *pantomimus,*
  dancer
imitābātur *was imitating, was*
  miming
mōtibus: mōtus *movement*
quasi *as if*
appellābant: appellāre *call*

statūrā: statūra *height*

interruptā: interrumpere
  interrupt

'audīte, ō scelestī!' clāmāvit Tychicus. 'vōs prāvī hunc hominem tamquam deum adōrātis. sunt tamen nūllī deī praeter ūnum! ūnus Deus sōlus adōrandus est! hunc Deum vērum quem plūrimī ignōrant, nunc vōbīs dēclārō.'

mussitāre coepērunt spectātōrēs. aliī rogāvērunt utrum 20
Tychicus iocōs faceret an īnsānīret; aliī servōs arcessīvērunt quī eum ex hortō ēicerent. Tychicus autem perstitit.

'Deus, ut prophētae nostrī nōbīs praedīxērunt, homō factus est et inter nōs habitāvit. aegrōs sānāvit; evangelium prōnūntiāvit; vītam aeternam nōbīs pollicitus est. tum in cruce 25
suffīxus, mortuus est et in sepulcrō positus est. sed tertiō diē resurrēxit et vīvus ā discipulīs suīs vīsus est. deinde in caelum ascendit, ubi et nunc rēgnat et in perpetuum rēgnābit.'

dum haec Tychicus dēclārat, servī Vitelliae signō datō eum comprehendērunt. domō eum trahēbant magnā vōce 30
clāmantem:

'mox Dominus noster, rēx glōriae, ad nōs reveniet; ē caelō dēscendet cum sonitū tubārum, magnō numerō angelōrum comitante. et vīvōs et mortuōs iūdicābit. nōs Chrīstiānī, sī vītam pūram vīxerimus et eī crēdiderimus, ad caelum ascendēmus. ibi 35
semper cum Dominō in pāce aeternā erimus. tū autem, Paris, fīlius diabolī, nisi vitiīs tuīs dēstiteris, poenās dabis. nūlla erit fuga. nam flammae, ē caelō missae, tē et omnēs scelestōs dēvorābunt.'

quae cum prōnūntiāvisset, Tychicus multīs verberibus 40
acceptīs domō ēiectus est. spectātōrum plūrimī eum vehementer dērīdēbant; paucī tamen, praesertim servī ac lībertī, tacēbant, quia Chrīstiānī erant ipsī.

praeter *except*
vērum: vērus *true*
dēclārō: dēclārāre *declare,*
  proclaim
mussitāre *murmur*
prophētae: prophēta *prophet*
praedīxērunt: praedīcere
  foretell, predict
evangelium *good news, gospel*
prōnūntiāvit: prōnūntiāre
  proclaim, preach
aeternam: aeternus *eternal*
pollicitus est *promised*
cruce: crux *cross*
suffīxus: suffīgere *nail, fasten*
resurrēxit: resurgere *rise again*
discipulīs: discipulus *disciple,*
  follower
caelum *sky, heaven*
rēgnat: rēgnāre *reign*
in perpetuum *for ever*
glōriae: glōria *glory*
angelōrum: angelus *angel*
comitante: comitāns
  accompanying
iūdicābit: iūdicāre *judge*
pūram: pūrus *pure*
erimus *shall be*
diabolī: diabolus *devil*
nisi *unless*
vitiīs: vitium *sin*
verberibus: verber *blow*

Christianity

Christianity originated in the Roman province of Judaea, where Jesus Christ was crucified in about AD 29. It may have reached Rome during the reign of the Emperor Claudius (AD 41–54). Saint Paul, who was brought to Rome under arrest in about AD 60, ends one of his letters from Rome by passing on messages of greeting from several Christians living in the city, including some who belong to 'Caesar's house' (the household of the emperor).

The early Christians believed that Jesus not only had risen from the dead and ascended into heaven, but would return again to earth in the fairly near future, in the way described by Tychicus on p. 80. The message of Christianity appealed mainly to the poor and the down-trodden, although it also attracted a few of the wealthy and nobly born.

At first the Romans tended to confuse Christianity with Judaism. This is not surprising, since both religions came from Judaea; also the Christians, like the Jews, believed that there was only one God and refused to acknowledge any other. For this reason they were disliked by the Romans; occasionally they were persecuted. The most famous persecution took place in AD 64 under the Emperor Nero, who treated the Christians as scapegoats for the great fire of Rome. They were condemned to be torn to pieces by wild beasts, or set alight as human torches.

But persecutions like these were not common; the Roman government usually preferred to leave the Christians alone. When Pliny, the Roman governor of Bithynia, asked the Emperor Trajan how he ought to deal with people accused of Christianity, Trajan replied:

'They are not to be hunted down: if they are brought before you and proved guilty, they must be punished, but if anyone says that he is *not* a Christian and proves it by saying a prayer to our Roman gods, he must go free, even if his previous behaviour has been very suspicious.'

The early Christians sometimes portrayed Christ as a beardless young man, like some of the Roman gods. The statue above may show him as an adolescent, perhaps debating with the priests in the Temple at Jerusalem. The mosaic below, from Hinton St Mary in Britain, shows the letters X and P behind Christ's head. These are the first two letters of 'Christ' in Greek, and were often used as a Christian symbol (as on the previous page).

in aulā Domitiānī

I

When you have read this part of the story, answer the questions on the next page.

in scaenā parvā, quae in aulae Domitiānī ātriō exstrūcta erat,
Paris fābulam dē amōre Mārtis et Veneris agēbat. simul pūmiliō,
Myropnous nōmine, tībīcen atque amīcus Paridis, suāviter tībiīs
cantābat. nūllī aderant spectātōrēs nisi Domitia Augusta, uxor
Imperātōris Domitiānī, quae Paridem inter familiārissimōs suōs   5
habēbat. oculīs in eō fīxīs fābulam intentē spectābat. tam
mīrābilis, tam perīta ars eius erat ut lacrimās retinēre Domitia
vix posset.

    subitō servus, nōmine Olympus, quem Domitia iānuam ātriī
custōdīre iusserat, ingressus est.   10

    'domina', inquit, 'ego Epaphrodītum, Augustī lībertum,
modo cōnspicātus sum trānseuntem āream, decem mīlitibus
comitantibus. mox hūc intrābit.'

    quibus verbīs audītīs, Paris ad Domitiam conversus rīsit.

Paris:	dēliciae meae! quam fortūnāta es! Epaphrodītus 15
	ipse, Augustī lībertus, tē vīsitāre cupit.
Domitia:	(*adventū Epaphrodītī commōta*) mī Pari, tibi
	perīculōsum est hīc manēre. odiō es Epaphrodītō! sī
	tē apud mē ille invēnerit, poenās certē dabis. iubēbit
	mīlitēs in carcerem tē conicere. fuge! 20
Paris:	cūr fugiendum est? illum psittacum Domitiānī
	haudquāquam timeō.
Domitia:	at ego valdē timeō. nam mihi quoque Epaphrodītus
	est inimīcus. iussū eius conclāvia mea saepe
	īnspiciuntur; epistulae meae leguntur; ancillae meae 25
	cotīdiē interrogantur. potestās eius nōn minor est
	quam Imperātōris ipsīus.
Paris:	mea columba, dēsine timēre! mē nōn capiet iste
	homunculus. paulīsper abībō.

haec locūtus, columnam proximam celeriter cōnscendit et per   30
compluvium ēgressus in tēctō sē cēlāvit. Myropnous quoque sē
cēlāre cōnstituit. post tapēte quod dē longuriō gravī pendēbat sē
collocāvit. Domitia contrā, quae quamquam perterrita erat in
lectō manēbat vultū compositō, Olympō imperāvit ut aliquōs
versūs recitāret.   35

---

simul *at the same time*
tībīcen *pipe player*
tībiīs cantābat: tībiīs cantāre
  play on the pipes
familiārissimōs: familiāris
  close friend

**Augustī lībertum: Augustī
lībertus** *freedman of
Augustus, freedman of the
emperor*

certē *certainly*

conclāvia: conclāve *room*
īnspiciuntur: īnspicere *search*

compluvium *compluvium
(opening in roof)*
tapēte *tapestry, wall-hanging*
longuriō: longurius *pole*
pendēbat: pendēre *hang*
contrā *on the other hand*
compositō: compositus
  composed, steady

Questions

		Marks

1 **in scaenā parvā** (line 1). Where had this stage been built? — 1

2 What story was Paris performing? — 1

3 Who was the pipe player supplying the musical accompaniment? Write down three things we are told about him. — 2

4 How many spectators were watching the performance? — 1

5 From lines 6–8 pick out:

   a One group of four words that show Domitia's attention was focused on Paris. — 1

   b Another group of words that show she was deeply affected by Paris' skill as an actor. — 1

6 What had Olympus been ordered to do? — 1

7 What news did he bring? — 3

8 **sī tē … tē conicere** (lines 18–20). Explain why Domitia thought it was dangerous for Paris to stay. — 3

9 **iussū eius … interrogantur** (lines 24–6). Domitia mentioned three ways in which Epaphroditus was making life unpleasant for her. What were they? — 3

10 Where did **a** Paris and **b** Myropnous hide? — 2

11 While Paris and Myropnous were hiding, where was Domitia? How did she try to pretend that everything was normal (lines 33–5)? — 1 + 2

12 Read lines 14–33 again. What picture have you formed of Paris' personality? Make three different points and refer to these lines to support each of them. — 3

TOTAL **25**

II

Olympō recitante, ingressus est Epaphrodītus. decem mīlitēs eum comitābantur.

Epaphrodītus: ubi est iste pantomīmus quem impudēns tū   **impudēns** *shameless*
                amās? ubi eum cēlāvistī?
Domitia: verba tua nōn intellegō. sōla sum, ut vidēs. hic   5
                servus mē versibus dēlectat, nōn Paris.
Epaphrodītus: *(conversus ad mīlitēs)* quaerite Paridem! festīnāte!
                omnia īnspicite conclāvia!

mīlitēs igitur conclāvia dīligentissimē īnspexērunt, sed frūstrā.
Paridem nusquam invenīre poterant.   *10*

Epaphrodītus: caudicēs! sī Paris effūgerit, vōs poenās dabitis.
                cūr tēctum nōn īnspexistis? ferte scālās!   **scālās: scālae** *ladders*

quae cum audīvisset Domitia palluit. Myropnous tamen, quī per
tapēte cautē prōspiciēbat, cōnsilium audācissimum cēpit. tapēte
lēniter manū movēre coepit. mox Epaphrodītus, dum ātrium   *15*
suspīciōsus circumspectat, mōtum tapētis vīdit.   **suspīciōsus** *suspicious*

Epaphrodītus: ecce! movētur tapēte! latebrās Paridis invēnī!   **latebrās: latebrae** *hiding-place*
                nunc illum capiam.

quibus dictīs, Epaphrodītus ad tapēte cum magnō clāmōre sē   **sē praecipitāvit: sē**
praecipitāvit. Myropnous haudquāquam perturbātus, ubi   *20*   **praecipitāre** *hurl oneself*
Epaphrodītus appropinquāvit, tapēte magnā vī dētrāxit. dēcidit   **perturbātus** *disturbed, alarmed*
tapēte, dēcidit longurius. Epaphrodītus, tapētī convolūtus atque   **dētrāxit: dētrahere** *pull down*
simul longuriō percussus, prōcubuit exanimātus. Myropnous   **convolūtus: convolvere**
exsultāns tībiīs cantāre coepit.   *entangle*
    Domitia, quae sē iam ex pavōre recēperat, ad mīlitēs in   *25*
ātrium cum scālīs regressōs conversa est. eōs iussit
Epaphrodītum extrahere. mīlitibus eum extrahentibus
Myropnous assem in labra eius quasi mortuī posuit. dēnique   **assem: as** *as (small coin)*
Paris per compluvium dēspiciēns Epaphrodītō ita valēdīxit: **dēspiciēns: dēspicere** *look*
    'hīc iacet Tiberius Claudius Epaphrodītus, Augustī lībertus,   *30*   *down*
longuriō strātus.'   **strātus: sternere** *lay low,*
                                                                                         flatten

About the language 1: future tense

1 Study the following examples:

> nōlī dēspērāre! amīcus meus tē **servābit**.
> *Don't give up! My friend **will save** you.*

> servī ad urbem heri iērunt; crās **revenient**.
> *The slaves went to the city yesterday; they **will come back** tomorrow.*

The words in **bold type** are in the future tense.

2 The first and second conjugations form their future tense in the following way:

first conjugation		*second conjugation*	
portābō	*I shall carry*	docēbō	*I shall teach*
portābis	*you will carry*	docēbis	*you will teach*
portābit	*s/he will carry*	docēbit	*s/he will teach*
portābimus	*we shall carry*	docēbimus	*we shall teach*
portābitis	*you will carry*	docēbitis	*you will teach*
portābunt	*they will carry*	docēbunt	*they will teach*

3 The third and fourth conjugations form their future tense in another way:

third conjugation		*fourth conjugation*	
traham	*I shall drag*	audiam	*I shall hear*
trahēs	*you will drag*	audiēs	*you will hear*
trahet	*s/he will drag*	audiet	*s/he will hear*
trahēmus	*we shall drag*	audiēmus	*we shall hear*
trahētis	*you will drag*	audiētis	*you will hear*
trahent	*they will drag*	audient	*they will hear*

4 Further examples:

a crās ad Graeciam nāvigābimus.
b ille mercātor est mendāx; tibi numquam pecūniam reddet.
c fuge! mīlitēs tē in carcerem conicient!
d dux noster est vir benignus, quī vōs omnēs līberābit.
e 'quid crās faciēs?' 'ad theātrum ībō.'
f laudābō; respondēbit; appropinquābunt; rīdēbitis.
g veniēmus; trādent; dīcam; dormiet.

5 The future tense of **sum** is as follows:

erō	*I shall be*	erimus	*we shall be*
eris	*you will be*	eritis	*you will be*
erit	*s/he will be*	erunt	*they will be*

Word patterns: diminutives

1   Study the form and meaning of the following nouns:

homō	*man*	homunculus	*little man*
servus	*slave*	servulus	*little slave*
ager	*field*	agellus	*little field, plot of land*
fīlia	*daughter*	fīliola	*little daughter*

The nouns in the right-hand pair of columns are known as diminutives.

2   Using the information above as a guide, complete the following table:

corpus	*body*	corpusculum	. . . .
liber	*book*	libellus	. . . .
gladius	. . . .	gladiolus	. . . .
versus	. . . .	versiculus	. . . .
fābula	. . . .	fābella	. . . .

3   Here are the diminutives of some familiar words. Give their meanings and the Latin words from which they are derived. Use the Vocabulary at the back of the book to help you if necessary.

   vīllula, nāvicula, cēnula, fīliolus, ponticulus.

4   Study the following nouns and their diminutives:

sporta	*basket*	sportula	(1) *little basket*
			(2) *gift for clients (named after the little basket in which it once used to be carried)*
cōdex (*often spelt* caudex)	(1) *piece of wood* (2) *someone with no more sense than a piece of wood, i.e. fool, blockhead*	cōdicillī	(1) *wooden writing-tablets* (2) *codicil (written instructions added to a will)*

5   Compare these different types of diminutives used in English:

   a small pig is a . . . .   a small bus is a . . . .
   a small owl is an . . . .   a short skirt is a . . . .
   a short book is a . . . .   a small cigar is a . . . .

Practising the language

1   Complete each sentence with the right participle. Then translate the sentence.

    a hīs verbīs . . . ., Paris aequō animō respondit. (audītīs, portātīs)
    b signō . . . ., servī Tychicum ēiēcērunt. (victō, datō)
    c nāve . . . ., mercātor dēspērābat. (āmissā, refectā)
    d clientibus . . . ., praecō iānuam clausit. (dīmissīs, dēpositīs)
    e equitibus . . . ., hostēs fūgērunt. (cōnspectīs, dēfēnsīs)
    f cēnā . . . ., Haterius amīcōs in triclīnium dūxit. (cōnsūmptā, parātā)

2   Translate the first sentence of each pair. Then complete the second sentence
    with the passive form of the verb to express the same idea. Use the table on
    p. 126 to help you. Finally, translate the second sentence.

    For example: hospitēs fābulam spectābant.
                   fābula ab hospitibus . . . .

    Translated and completed, this becomes:

              hospitēs fābulam spectābant.
              The guests were watching the play.

              fābula ab hospitibus spectābātur.
              The play was being watched by the guests.

    In sentences **a–c**, the verbs are in the *imperfect* tense:

    a servī amphorās portābant.
        amphorae ā servīs . . . .
    b Salvius Haterium dēcipiēbat.
        Haterius ā Salviō . . . .
    c barbarī horreum oppugnābant.
        horreum ā barbarīs . . . .

    In sentences **d–f**, the verbs are in the *present* tense:

    d rhētor puerōs docet.
        puerī ā rhētore . . . .
    e aliquis iānuam aperit.
        iānua ab aliquō . . . .
    f centuriō mīlitēs cōnsistere iubet.
        mīlitēs ā centuriōne cōnsistere . . . .

About the language 2: future perfect tense

1 Study the following example:

> sī tē audīverō, respondēbō.
> *If I hear you, I shall reply.*

The replying takes place in the future, so Latin uses the future tense (**respondēbō**). The hearing also takes place in the future, but at a different time: hearing comes before replying. To indicate this difference in time, Latin uses an unusual tense known as the future perfect (**audīverō**).

2 Literally **audīverō** means *I shall have heard*, but it is often translated by an English present tense, as in the example above.

3 The forms of the future perfect are as follows:

portāverō	portāverimus
portāveris	portāveritis
portāverit	portāverint

4 Further examples:

a sī Epaphrodītus nōs cōnspexerit, tē interficiet.
b sī dīligenter quaesīveris, pecūniam inveniēs.
c sī servī bene labōrāverint, eīs praemium dabō.
d sī mīlitēs vīderō, fugiam.

A picture made from pieces of coloured marbles, showing the procession at the start of the chariot races. The patron of the games, perhaps an emperor, drives a two-horse chariot. Behind him are riders in the colours of the four teams, red, blue, green and white.

Entertainment

The theatre

Throughout the first century AD, the three theatres in Rome regularly provided popular entertainment at festival time. But there was a change in the kind of drama presented.

The traditional type of tragedy was losing its popularity and being replaced by pantomime. A pantomime had only one actor; he was known as a **pantomīmus** (acting everything) because he acted all the parts in the story, changing his mask as he changed characters. For example, a pantomimus who was presenting the love-affair of Mars and Venus would take the parts not only of Mars and Venus themselves but also of Helios the sun-god telling Venus' husband Vulcan about the affair, Vulcan setting a trap for the guilty pair, and the other gods coming one by one to look at Mars and Venus when they were caught in the act.

The pantomimus did not speak, but danced and mimed rather in the manner of a modern ballet dancer, and was often accompanied by an orchestra and a chorus who sang the words of the story. The story itself was usually based on Greek myth but sometimes on history. The pantomimus represented the story's action with graceful movements and gestures; he needed plenty of physical skill and stamina, as well as an attractive appearance and a wide knowledge of literature. One of the most famous of all pantomimi was the dancer Paris, who appears in the stories of Stages 33 and 34.

In the same way that pantomimes were replacing tragedies, comedies were being replaced by mimes. A mime was a crude slapstick farce, usually on a theme taken from everyday life. The style of performance was generally obscene or grotesque or both.

Above: *An ivory carving showing a pantomime performer with the masks and props of three characters.*
Below: *Although this picture may show an actor in tragedy rather than pantomime, it gives a good idea of the flowing robes and the masks Paris wore.*

Chariot-racing

The most popular form of public entertainment in Rome, however, was undoubtedly chariot-racing. Almost everybody, from the emperor downwards, took an interest in this sport. The Circus Maximus, where the most important chariot-racing took place, could hold 250,000 spectators – a far higher capacity than any modern football or baseball stadium. Much money changed hands in betting, and each of the rival chariot-teams was cheered on by its fans with passionate enthusiasm.

There were four teams (**factiōnēs**) competing regularly with each other: green, blue, red and white. Each team consisted of one, two or three chariots, and the commonest number of horses to a chariot was four. A day's programme normally consisted of twenty-four races, each lasting seven laps (about 5 miles) and taking about a quarter of an hour to run. Seven huge eggs of marble or wood were hoisted high above the central platform (**spīna**), and every time the chariots completed a lap, one egg was lowered. Likewise seven bronze dolphins dived in turn to mark the laps. The charioteer had to race at full speed down the length of the circus and then display his greatest skill at the turning-point (**mēta**); if he took the bend too slowly he would be overtaken, and if he took it too fast he might crash. He raced with the reins tied tightly round his body, and in his belt he carried a knife; if he crashed, his life might depend on how quickly he could cut himself free from the wreckage.

Gladiatorial fights

Another centre of entertainment was the Flavian amphitheatre, later known as the Colosseum. Up to 50,000 spectators could watch the gladiatorial combats and beast-hunts that took place here. Occasionally, the arena was filled with water for the representation of sea battles. (For information about gladiatorial shows see Book I, Stage 8, pp. 107–10.)

A 'Thracian' gladiator. His helmet is decorated with feathers and a griffin's head.

Private entertainment

Not all entertainment was public. Rich Romans enjoyed presenting private shows of various kinds, as in the story on pp. 79–80, where Paris performs in Haterius' garden for Vitellia and her friends. One elderly lady, Ummidia Quadratilla, kept her own private troupe of pantomimi. Often entertainment would be presented at a dinner-party. This might consist of dancing-girls, freaks, actors, jugglers, acrobats, a band of musicians, a novelty like the philosopher Euphrosyne, or a trained slave reciting a poem or other literary work – possibly written by the host, which might sometimes be rather embarrassing for the guests. The more serious types of entertainment were often put on by highly educated hosts for equally cultivated and appreciative guests; but they might sometimes, like Euphrosyne's philosophy lecture, be presented by ignorant and uninterested hosts who merely wanted to be fashionable or were trying to pass themselves off as persons of good taste and culture.

An acrobat doing a handstand on a crocodile.

Two scenes at the Circus Maximus

Study these two pictures of chariot racing.

In the top picture:
1 The charioteer on the left has fallen from his chariot. Why might this accident have happened?
2 What urgent action must he take now?
3 What is the purpose of the row of dolphins in the background?

In the bottom picture:
4 It has been suggested that the charioteer on the left is reining in the inside horse. Why would he do this?
5 The charioteer on the right seems to be whipping up his team. Why can he now drive them faster?

Two terracotta plaques showing chariot racing at the Circus Maximus.

Vocabulary checklist 33

appellō, appellāre, appellāvī,
   appellātus   *call, call out to*
at   *but*
brevis, breve   *short, brief*
coniciō, conicere, coniēcī,
   coniectus   *hurl, throw*
contrā   *against, on the other hand*
crās   *tomorrow*
dēcidō, dēcidere, dēcidī   *fall down*
dēscendō, dēscendere, dēscendī   *come down, go down*
ēiciō, ēicere, ēiēcī, ēiectus   *throw out*
et ... et   *both ... and*
excipiō, excipere, excēpī,
   exceptus   *receive*
fuga, fugae   *escape*
hīc   *here*
lūdus, lūdī   *game*
moveō, movēre, mōvī, mōtus   *move*
nisi   *except, unless*
numerus, numerī   *number*
potestās, potestātis   *power*
quia   *because*
reficiō, reficere, refēcī, refectus   *repair*
rēgīna, rēgīnae   *queen*
utrum   *whether*
vērus, vēra, vērum   *true, real*
   rē vērā   *in fact, truly, really*

Coin of the Emperor Titus,
celebrating the opening of
the Colosseum.

LIBERTUS

STAGE 34

ultiō Epaphrodītī

Epaphrodītus, ā Paride atque Domitiā ēlūsus, eōs ulcīscī
vehementissimē cupiēbat. Imperātor quoque, īrā et suspīciōne
commōtus, Epaphrodītum saepe hortābātur ut Paridem
Domitiamque pūnīret. Epaphrodītō tamen difficile erat
Domitiam, uxōrem Imperātōris, et Paridem, pantomīmum   5
nōtissimum, apertē accūsāre. auxilium igitur ab amīcō Salviō
petīvit.

    Epaphrodītus 'nōn modo ego', inquit, 'sed etiam Imperātor
Paridem Domitiamque pūnīre cupit. sī mē in hāc rē adiūveris,
magnum praemium tibi dabitur.'   10

    Salvius, rē paulīsper cōgitātā, tranquillē respondit:

    'cōnfīde mihi, amīce; ego tibi rem tōtam administrābō.
īnsidiae parābuntur; Domitia et Paris in īnsidiās ēlicientur; ambō
capientur et pūnientur.'

    'quid Domitiae accidet?' rogāvit Epaphrodītus.   15

    'Domitia accūsābitur; damnābitur; fortasse relēgābitur.'

    'et Paris?'

    Salvius rīsit.

    'ēmovēbitur.'

ēlūsus: ēlūdere *trick, outwit*
ulcīscī *to take revenge on*
suspīciōne: suspīciō *suspicion*

ēlicientur: ēlicere *lure, entice*

relēgābitur: relēgāre *exile*

Epaphroditus

Epaphroditus was a former slave of the Emperor Nero. Under Domitian, Epaphroditus' official title was secretary **ā libellīs** (in charge of petitions – the word **ā** has an unusual meaning in this phrase), which means that he helped the emperor to deal with the various petitions or requests submitted to him by groups and individuals. The opportunities for bribery are obvious, and imperial freedmen like him were widely unpopular.

The large block of marble below is part of an inscription honouring him. The top line tells us he is the emperor's freedman: [A]VG L stands for **Augustī lībertus**. The bottom line boasts of gold crowns (**corōnīs aureīs**) he has been awarded, possibly as a reward for the part he played in unmasking a conspiracy against Nero.

When he eventually fell out of favour with Domitian, he was executed on the grounds that he had helped Nero to commit suicide twenty-seven years before.

*Epaphroditus wearing the toga, the mark of a citizen. When he was freed he gained the right to wear it. On the table is his **pilleus**, the cap of liberty he was given to mark his manumission.*

īnsidiae

I

When you have read this part of the story, answer the questions at the end.

paucīs post diēbus Domitia ancillam, nōmine Chionēn, ad sē
vocāvit.

'epistulam', inquit, 'ā Vitelliā, uxōre Hateriī, missam modo
accēpī. ēheu! Vitellia in morbum gravem incidit. statim mihi
vīsitanda est. tē volō omnia parāre.'   5

tum Chionē, ē cubiculō dominae ēgressa, iussit lectīcam
parārī et servōs arcessī. medicum quoque quaesīvit quī
medicāmenta quaedam Vitelliae parāret. inde Domitia lectīcā
vecta, comitantibus servīs ancillāque, domum Hateriī profecta
est. difficile erat eīs per viās prōgredī, quod nox obscūra erat   10
multumque pluēbat.

cum domum Hateriī pervēnissent, iānuam apertam
invēnērunt. servīs extrā iānuam relictīs, Domitia cum Chionē
ingressa est. spectāculum mīrābile eīs ingredientibus obiectum
est. ātrium magnificē ōrnātum erat: ubīque lūcēbant lucernae,   15
corōnae rosārum dē omnibus columnīs pendēbant. sed omnīnō
dēsertum erat ātrium. inde fēminae, triclīnium ingressae, id
quoque dēsertum vīdērunt. in mediō tamen cēna sūmptuōsa
posita erat: mēnsae epulīs exquīsītissimīs cumulātae erant,

Chionēn *Greek accusative of*
Chionē

parārī *to be prepared*
arcessī *to be summoned, to be
sent for*
medicāmenta:
   medicāmentum *medicine,
   drug*

eīs … obiectum est *met them,
was presented to them*

epulīs: epulae *dishes*
cumulātae erant: cumulāre
   heap

pōcula vīnō optimō plēna erant. quibus vīsīs, ancilla timidā   20
vōce,

'cavendum est nōbīs', inquit. 'aliquid mīrī hīc agitur.'

'fortasse Vitellia morbō affecta est cum cēnāret. sine dubiō
iam in cubiculō iacet', respondit Domitia, ignāra īnsidiārum
quās Salvius parāverat.   25

cavendum est: cavēre *beware*
mīrī: mīrus *extraordinary*

Questions

		Marks
1	What did Domitia tell Chione (lines 3–4)?	2
2	What was said to have happened to Vitellia?	1
3	What did Domitia decide must be done at once?	1
4	What preparations did Chione make (lines 6–8)?	2 + 2
5	Where were Domitia and her party going?	1
6	Why was their journey difficult?	2
7	What did Domitia and Chione discover at the entrance?	1
8	What happened to the slaves (line 13)?	1
9	**ātrium magnificē ōrnātum est** (line 15). In what ways did the atrium look particularly splendid?	2
10	What was odd about the atrium and the dining-room?	1
11	Why is the dinner described as **sūmptuōsa** (line 18)?	2
12	What did Chione say about the situation (line 22)?	2
13	What explanation did Domitia give? What did she think Vitellia was now doing?	2 + 1
14	Which two Latin words show that Domitia was unaware of what was going on?	1
15	What do you think will happen next?	1

TOTAL **25**

II

itaque per domum dēsertam, ancillā timidē sequente, Domitia
prōgredī coepit. cum ad cubiculum ubi Vitellia dormīre solēbat
pervēnisset, in līmine cōnstitit. cubiculum erat obscūrum.
Chionēn ad triclīnium remīsit quae lucernam ferret. in silentiō
noctis diū exspectābat dum redīret ancilla. haec tamen nōn   5
rediit. tandem Domitia morae impatiēns in cubiculum irrūpit.
vacuum erat. tum dēmum pavōre magnō perturbāta est.
tenebrae, silentium, ancillae absentia, haec omnia perīculī
indicia esse vidēbantur. scīlicet falsa erat epistula!

Domitia ad aulam quam celerrimē regredī cōnstituit   10
priusquam aliquid malī sibi accideret. dum per ātrium vacuum
fugit, vōce hominis subitō perterrita est.

remīsit: remittere *send back*
dum *until*
morae impatiēns *impatient at the delay*
vacuum: vacuus *empty*
tum dēmum *then at last, only then*
absentia *absence*
vidēbantur: vidērī *seem*

'dēliciae meae, salvē! tūne quoque ad cēnam invītāta es?'
tum vōcem agnōvit.

'mī Pari', inquit, 'īnsidiae, nōn cēna, nōbīs parātae sunt.   15
effugiendum nōbīs est, dum possumus.'

exitium

exitium *ruin, destruction*

I

Domitiā haec dīcente, Myropnous, quī dominum comitātus erat,
ad iānuam contendit. cautē prōspexit. ecce! via tōta mīlitibus
praetōriānīs plēna erat. neque lectīca, neque ancilla, neque servī
usquam vidērī poterant.

   ad ātrium reversus Myropnous 'āctum est dē nōbīs!'   5
exclāmāvit. 'appropinquant praetōriānī! mox hūc ingredientur!'

   hōc tamen cognitō, Paris 'nōlī dēspērāre', inquit. 'cōnsilium
habeō. Myropnū, tibi iānua custōdienda est. prohibē mīlitēs
ingredī. sī mē vel Domitiam in hōc locō cēperint, certē nōs
interficient. cōnandum est nōbīs per postīcum ēlābī.'   10

   Myropnous igitur iānuam claudere contendit. quō factō,
sellās ex ātriō, lectōs ē cubiculīs proximīs raptim in faucēs
trahere coepit. brevī ingēns pyra exstrūcta est.

   mīlitēs praetōriānī, cum iānuam clausam cōnspexissent,
haesitantēs cōnstitērunt. sed tribūnus, nē Paris et Domitia   15
effugerent, iānuam effringī iussit. statim iānua secūribus
pulsābātur. Myropnous ubi sonitum pulsantium audīvit pyram
incendit. amphoram oleī ē culīnā portāvit quā flammās augēret.
tum pyrā flagrante, amīcōs sequī contendit.

praetōriānīs: praetōriānus
   praetorian (belonging to the
   emperor's bodyguard)
usquam *anywhere*
reversus: revertī *return*
āctum est dē nōbīs *it's all over*
   with us, we're done for
postīcum *back gate*
ēlābī *slip out, escape*
faucēs *passage, entrance-way*
pyra *pyre*

secūribus: secūris *axe*

oleī: oleum *oil*
flagrante: flagrāre *blaze*

II

Paris et Domitia, ubi ad postīcum pervēnērunt, duōs mīlitēs ibi
positōs invēnērunt. quōs cum vīdissent, quamquam Domitia
omnīnō dē salūte dēspērābat, Paris in hōc discrīmine
audācissimum atque callidissimum sē praestitit. nam cēlātā
haud procul Domitiā, ipse per postīcum audācter prōgressus sē   5
mīlitibus ostendit. tum quasi fugiēns, retrō in hortum cucurrit.

   statim clāmāvērunt mīlitēs: 'ecce Paris! Paris effugere
cōnātur!'

   mīlitibus sequentibus, Paris per hortum modo hūc modo illūc
ruēbat. post statuās sē cēlābat mīlitēsque vōce blandā dērīdēbat.   10
illī incertī ubi esset pantomīmus, vōcem Paridis circā hortum
sequēbantur.

retrō *back*

modo … modo *now … now*

circā *around*

tandem audīvit Paris sonitum cēterōrum mīlitum domum
irrumpentium. iussū tribūnī flammae celeriter exstīnctae sunt.
brevī tōta domus mīlitibus plēna erat. dēnique Paris intellēxit
quantō in perīculō esset sed etiam tum haudquāquam
dēspērāvit.

    mediō in hortō stābat arbor veterrima, quae tēctō domūs
imminēbat. simulatque intrāvērunt mīlitēs hortum, arborem
Paris cōnscendit. hinc prōsilīre in tēctum cōnātus est. prōsiluit,
sed tēgulae tēctī lūbricae erant. paulīsper in margine tēctī stetit;
deinde praeceps humum lāpsus est.

    intereā Domitia, quae per postīcum nūllō vidente ēgressa
erat, prope vīllam manēbat dum Paris ad sē venīret. lāpsō tamen
corpore eius, tantus erat fragor ut etiam ad aurēs Domitiae
advenīret. quae metū āmēns vītaeque suae neglegēns in hortum
reversa est. ubi corpus Paridis humī iacēns vīdit, dolōre cōnfecta
sē in eum coniēcit eīque ōscula multa dedit.

    'valē, dēliciae meae, valē!'

    adiit tribūnus. Domitiam ad aulam dēdūcī iussit. ipse caput
pantomīmī amputātum ad Epaphrodītum rettulit.

15

20

25

30

exstīnctae sunt: exstinguere
   extinguish

arbor *tree*

prōsilīre *jump*
tēgulae: tēgula *tile*
lūbricae: lūbricus *slippery*
margine: margō *edge*
nūllō (*used as ablative of* **nēmō**)
   no one
fragor *crash*
āmēns *out of her mind, in a*
   frenzy
cōnfecta: cōnfectus *overcome*

amputātum: amputāre *cut off*

About the language 1: present passive infinitive

1   In Stage 13, you met sentences containing infinitives:

currere volō.   servī **labōrāre** nōn possunt.
I want to run.   *The slaves are not able to work*.
                Or, The slaves cannot work.

This kind of infinitive is known in full as the present active infinitive.

2   In Stage 34, you have met another kind of infinitive:

volō epistulam **recitārī**.   Paris **invenīrī** nōn poterat.
I want the letter to be read out.   *Paris was unable to be found*.
                        Or, Paris could not be found.

This infinitive is known as the present passive infinitive.

3   Compare the following examples of present active and present passive infinitives:

	present active		*present passive*	
first conjugation	portāre	*to carry*	portārī	*to be carried*
second conjugation	docēre	*to teach*	docērī	*to be taught*
third conjugation	trahere	*to drag*	trahī	*to be dragged*
fourth conjugation	audīre	*to hear*	audīrī	*to be heard*

4   Further examples of the present passive infinitive:

a   volō iānuam aperīrī.
b   dux iussit captīvum līberārī.
c   fūr capī nōlēbat.
d   neque Vitellia neque ancilla vidērī poterat.
e   Haterius vīnum statim effundī iussit.

5   Deponent verbs form their infinitive in the following way:

first conjugation	cōnārī	*to try*
second conjugation	pollicērī	*to promise*
third conjugation	sequī	*to follow*
fourth conjugation	orīrī	*to rise*

Note that the infinitive has a passive ending, but an active meaning.

Further examples:

a   tribūnus iussit mīlitēs pantomīmum sequī.
b   aegrōtī deam precārī volēbant.
c   mercātor tandem proficīscī cōnstituit.
d   puerī tam perterritī erant ut loquī nōn possent.
e   hostēs ē castrīs ēgredī nōlēbant.

honōrēs

Salviō aulam intrantī obviam iit Epaphrodītus. cōmiter excēpit.

Epaphrodītus:	mī Salvī, quālis artifex es! tuā arte iste	**artifex** *artist*
	pantomīmus occīsus est. tuā arte Domitia ex	
	Ītaliā relēgāta est. Imperātor, summō gaudiō	
	affectus, spectāculum splendidissimum in 5	
	amphitheātrō Flāviō darī iussit. crās diēs fēstus	
	ab omnibus cīvibus celebrābitur; puerī	
	puellaeque deōrum effigiēs corōnīs flōrum	
	ōrnābunt; sacerdōtēs sacrificia offerent; ingēns	
	cīvium multitūdō Imperātōrem ad templum 10	**dīs = deīs: deus** *god*
	Iovis comitābitur, ubi ille dīs immortālibus	**cūriam: cūria** *senate-house*
	grātiās aget. mox senātōrēs ad cūriam fēstīs	
	vestīmentīs prōgredientur et Domitiānō	**morandum est: morārī** *delay*
	grātulābuntur. venī mēcum! nōn morandum est	
	nōbīs. Imperātor enim nōs exspectat. mihi 15	**ōrnāmenta praetōria** *honorary*
	ōrnāmenta praetōria, tibi cōnsulātum prōmīsit.	*praetorship, honorary rank of*
Salvius:	cōnsulātum mihi prōmīsit? quam fortūnātus	*praetor*
	sum!	
Epaphrodītus:	venī! Imperātōrī grātiās agere dēbēmus.	

Epaphrodītō et Salviō ēgressīs ut Domitiānum salūtārent, ē   20
latebrīs rēpsit Myropnous. nunc dēnique intellēxit quis esset
auctor exitiī Paridis. lacrimīs effūsīs, indignam amīcī mortem   **auctor** *person responsible*
lūgēbat. manibus ad caelum sublātīs nōmen Salviī dētestātus est.   **indignam: indignus**
tum tībiās āmēns frēgit, haec verba locūtus: *unworthy, undeserved*
    'ego numquam iterum tībiīs cantābō priusquam perierit   25   **sublātīs (*past participle*): tollere**
Salvius.'   *raise, lift up*
      priusquam perierit *until …*
      perishes

Tombstone of a dwarf pipe player called Myropnous.

About the language 2: future passive tense

1 Study the following examples:

> crās nūntiī ad rēgem **mittentur**.
> *Tomorrow messengers will be sent to the king.*

> cēna sūmptuōsa ā servīs **parābitur**.
> *An expensive dinner will be prepared by slaves.*

The words in **bold type** are passive forms of the future tense.

2 Compare the following active and passive forms:

	future active	*future passive*
first conjugation	portābit	portābitur
	s/he will carry	*s/he will be carried*
	portābunt	portābuntur
	they will carry	*they will be carried*
third conjugation	trahet	trahētur
	s/he will drag	*s/he will be dragged*
	trahent	trahentur
	they will drag	*they will be dragged*

3 Further examples:

a ingēns praemium victōrī dabitur.
b Paris mox capiētur.
c omnēs vīllae dēlēbuntur.
d illī custōdēs quī in statiōne dormīvērunt sevērissimē pūnientur.
e ūnus captīvus līberābitur, cēterī occīdentur.

4 Notice how the future tense of deponent verbs is formed:

first conjugation	cōnābitur	*s/he will try*
	cōnābuntur	*they will try*
third conjugation	loquētur	*s/he will speak*
	loquentur	*they will speak*

Further examples:

a mīlitēs crās proficīscentur.
b dominus meus, quī stultissimus est, nihil suspicābitur.
c sōl mox oriētur.
d multī senātōrēs Domitiānum ad forum comitābuntur.
e sī inimīcus tuus hoc venēnum cōnsūmpserit, moriētur.

Word patterns: compound verbs 3

1 You are now familiar with the way compound verbs are formed. Here are some further examples:

adīre	*to go towards*	advenīre	*to come towards*
convenīre	*to come together, meet*	compōnere	*to put together, compose*

2 Now complete the following table:

prōpōnere	*to put forward*	prōmovēre	. . . .
trānsīre	. . . .	trānscurrere	. . . .
perrumpere	*to break through*	persecāre	. . . .

3 The words in **bold type** in the following sentences are derived from Latin compound verbs. Explain the link between the Latin verbs and their English derivatives.

   a At last she got the **promotion** she deserved.
   b The television **transmitter** broke down because of the storm.
   c In many cultures there are festivals to celebrate the **advent** of spring.

4 The meaning of a compound verb is not always obvious, even if you know both its parts.

   For example: **perīre** *to perish*; **āmittere** *to lose*; **condūcere** *to hire*.

Practising the language

1   Complete each sentence with the right form of the verb. Then translate the
    sentence.

    a   ego vōbīs rem tōtam . . . . (nārrābō, nārrābimus)
    b   amīcī meī cibum vestīmentaque nōbīs . . . . (praebēbit,
        praebēbunt)
    c   Imperātor spectāculum splendidum in amphitheātrō crās . . . .
        (dabunt, dabit)
    d   vōs estis fortiōrēs quam illī barbarī; eōs facile . . . . (superābitis,
        superābis)
    e   tū in vīllā manē; nōs per pōsticum . . . . (effugiam, effugiēmus)
    f   caudex! mē numquam . . . . (capiēs, capiētis)
    g   ego sum probus; tibi pecūniam . . . . (reddēmus, reddam)
    h   fugite! hostēs mox . . . . (aderunt, aderit)

2   Translate each English sentence into Latin by selecting correctly from the list
    of Latin words.

    a   *Many flowers were being thrown by the spectators.*
        | multa | flōris | ā spectātōribus | iactābant |
        | multī | flōrēs | inter spectātōrēs | iactābantur |

    b   *They warned my friend not to cross the bridge.*
        | amīcum | meīs | monuerant | nē | pōns | trānsīret |
        | amīcōs | meum | monuērunt | ut | pontem | trānsībat |

    c   *Having been ordered by the leader, we carried out the body.*
        | ad ducem | iussus | corpus | extulī |
        | ā duce | iussī | corporum | extulimus |

    d   *We saw the man whose brother you (s.) had arrested.*
        | hominem | quī | frāter | comprehenderātis | vidēmus |
        | hominum | cuius | frātrem | comprehenderās | vīdimus |

    e   *When the soldiers had been drawn up, I gave the centurion a sign.*
        | mīlitibus | īnstrūctīs | centuriōnem | signum | dedī |
        | mīlitēs | īnstrūctōs | centuriōnī | signō | dedit |

3 Translate the first sentence of each pair. Then complete the second sentence with the passive form of the verb. Use the table on p. 127 to help you. Finally, translate the second sentence.

For example: centuriō fūrēs vulnerāverat.
                      fūrēs ā centuriōne . . . .

Translated and completed, this becomes:

> centuriō fūrēs vulnerāverat.
> *The centurion had wounded the thieves.*

> fūrēs ā centuriōne vulnerātī erant.
> *The thieves had been wounded by the centurion.*

The perfect and pluperfect tenses are both used in this exercise. The verbs in sentences **a–e** are all first conjugation like **portō**.

a coquus cibum parāverat.
      cibus ā coquō . . . .
b mercātor latrōnēs superāverat.
      latrōnēs ā mercātōre . . . .
c dominī servōs laudāvērunt.
      servī ā dominīs . . . .
d clientēs patrōnum salūtāvērunt.
      patrōnus ā clientibus . . . .
e rēx mē ipsum accūsāvit.
      ego ipse ā rēge . . . .
f custōs magnum clāmōrem audīvit.
      magnus clāmor ā custōde . . . .

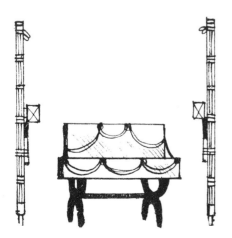

Left: *The consular chair and fasces which were the symbol of the consulship as promised to Salvius in the story* **honōrēs**. *The fasces were bundles of rods and axes, to symbolise the consul's power to order beatings and executions. They were carried for him by a procession of twelve lictors; the statuette on the right shows one of them.*

Freedmen

When a slave was set free (manumitted), he ceased to be the property of his master and became a **lībertus** instead of a **servus**. He also, as we have seen (pp. 56–7), became a **cliēns** of his ex-master, and his ex-master was now his **patrōnus**.

In addition, a freedman became a Roman citizen. He now had three names, of which the first two came from the name of his ex-master. (For example, Tiro, the freedman of Marcus Tullius Cicero, became Marcus Tullius Tiro.) As a citizen, he now had the right to vote in elections and to make a will or business agreement which would be valid in the eyes of the law. He could also get married. If he had been living in an unofficial marriage with a slave-woman, one of his first acts after manumission might be to save up enough money to buy her out of slavery and marry her legally.

There were some limits to the rights and privileges of a freedman, compared with other Roman citizens. He could not become a senator or **eques**, except by special favour of the emperor (and a freedwoman could not become a senator's wife). He could not serve in the legions, nor stand as a candidate in elections. One privilege, however, was available to a freedman. He could become one of the six priests (**sēvirī Augustālēs**) who were appointed in many Italian towns to look after the worship of the deified Emperor Augustus. Like all priesthoods, the priesthood of Augustus was a position of honour and prestige.

The law laid down certain obligations which a freedman owed to his ex-master. For example, a freedman was supposed to leave money to his ex-master in his will (ex-masters did not often insist on this); he was forbidden to do anything that would bring harm to his ex-master; and he had to do a certain number of days' work for his ex-master every year, or pay him a sum of money instead. It is clear from this that it would often be financially worthwhile for a master to manumit a slave; he would still be able to make some use of the ex-slave's services, but would no longer have to provide and pay for his food, clothing and shelter.

After manumission, a freedman had to put up with a certain amount of prejudice from those who despised him for having been a slave. He was also faced with the need to earn a living. His ex-master might help by providing money to start a small business, as Quintus did for Clemens in Stage 18, or introducing him to potential customers. Many highly skilled or educated freedmen were quickly able to earn a good living because they already possessed some special ability or experience; for example, a freedman might already be a skilled craftsman, teacher, musician or secretary, or be experienced in accountancy,

Relief showing two freedmen being manumitted. Although they both wear the cap of freedom, one kneels to his master, implying that he still has obligations to him.

Augustales

To be chosen as an Augustalis, or priest of the emperor, was the greatest honour open to many freedmen.
Top left: The hall in Herculaneum where the Augustales would meet to conduct worship and for ceremonial dinners.
Below left: Part of the inscription from a tomb at Pompeii, put up by a freedman for himself and his patroness, Vesonia. Notice how he must have been made an Augustalis after he had had the tomb built, because the word has been awkwardly squeezed in by a different letter-cutter. The honour, when it came, was too important to leave out of Vesonius Phileros' tomb inscription.

trade or banking. Freedmen who had previously used these skills in their master's service could now use them for their own benefit. There was plenty of demand for such services, and not much competition from freeborn Romans, who often lacked the necessary skills or regarded such work as below their dignity.

It is not surprising, therefore, that many freedmen became rich and successful, and a few freedmen became very rich indeed. The Vettii brothers, who set up their own business in Pompeii and eventually owned one of the most splendid houses in the town, are good examples of successful freedmen. But perhaps the most famous example of a wealthy freedman is a fictitious one: Trimalchio, the vulgar millionaire in Petronius' novel *Satyrica*. The story **cēna Haterii** in Stage 32 is partly based on Petronius' account of Trimalchio's dinner-party.

Some freedmen continued to live in their ex-master's household, doing the same work that they had done as slaves. One such man was Pliny's talented freedman Zosimus, who was equally skilled at reciting, lyre-playing and comedy-acting.

Pliny treated Zosimus with kindness and affection, and when Zosimus fell ill with tuberculosis, Pliny arranged a holiday abroad for him.

Further evidence of friendly relationships between ex-masters and freedmen comes from the large number of inscriptions, particularly on tombstones, that refer to freedmen and freedwomen. Sometimes, for example, freedmen set up tombstones in honour of their ex-masters:

> D M
> T. FLAVIO HOMERO T.
> FLAVIVS HYACINTHVS
> PATRONO BENE MERENTI

DM = dīs mānibus *to the spirits of the departed*
bene merentī: bene merēns *well deserving, deserving kindness*

Sometimes ex-masters set up tombstones to their favourite freedmen:

> D M
> IVLIO VITALI
> PATRONVS LIBERTO
> BENE MERENTI

Some ex-masters allowed freedmen and freedwomen to be buried with them in their tombs:

> D M
> TITVS FLAVIVS EV
> MOLPVS ET FLAVIA
> QVINTA SIBI FECE
> RVNT ET LIBERTIS LI
> BERTABVSQVE POS
> TERISQVE EORVM

lībertābus: līberta *freedwoman*
posterīs: posterī *future generations, descendants*

An ex-master might marry his freedwoman:

> D M
> T. FLAVIVS CERIALIS
> FLAVIAE PHILAENIDI
> LIBERTAE IDEM
> ET COIVGI
> B M F

idem et *here = and also*
coiugī = coniugī: coniūnx *wife*
BMF = bene merentī fēcit

A small but very important group of freedmen worked as personal assistants to the emperor. As slaves, they had been known as **servī Caesaris**, and as freedmen they were known as **lībertī Augustī**. ('Caesar' and 'Augustus' were both used as titles of the emperor.) One of these men was Epaphroditus, who worked first for Nero and later for Domitian.

As we have seen, Epaphroditus was the emperor's secretary **ā libellīs**, in charge of petitions. Other freedmen of the emperor were in charge of correspondence (**ab epistulīs**) and accounts (**ā ratiōnibus**). They all worked closely with the emperor in the day-to-day running of government business.

Under some emperors, especially Claudius and Nero, these freedmen became immensely rich and powerful. They were often bitterly resented by the Roman nobles and senators. This resentment can be seen very plainly in two letters which Pliny wrote about Pallas, the secretary **ā ratiōnibus** of the Emperor Claudius. Pallas had been awarded the **ōrnāmenta praetōria** (honorary praetorship) like Epaphroditus in the story on p. 101. This means he was given the various privileges normally possessed by a praetor: special dress, special seat at public ceremonies, special funeral after death, and so on. Even though this had happened fifty years previously, Pliny is boiling with anger. He describes Pallas as a **furcifer**, and much else besides. His outburst shows very clearly how much ill-feeling could be caused by an emperor's use of ex-slaves as important and powerful assistants in running the empire.

The Emperor Domitian's vast palace on the Palatine hill overlooking the Circus Maximus. This picture shows part of the emperor's personal quarters, centred on a garden with the remains of a large fountain.

Vocabulary checklist 34

accūsō, accūsāre, accūsāvī,
  accūsātus   *accuse*
auctor, auctōris   *creator, originator, person*
                                        responsible
  mē auctōre   *at my suggestion*
dum   *while, until*
frangō, frangere, frēgī, frāctus   *break*
gaudium, gaudiī   *joy*
haud   *not*
modo   *just*
priusquam   *before, until*
procul   *far off*
quasi   *as if*
sine   *without*
sonitus, sonitūs   *sound*
vel   *or*
vestīmenta, vestīmentōrum   *clothes*

Deponent verbs

adipīscor, adipīscī, adeptus sum   *obtain*
comitor, comitārī, comitātus sum   *accompany*
cōnor, cōnārī, cōnātus sum   *try*
cōnspicor, cōnspicārī,
  cōnspicātus sum   *catch sight of*
ēgredior, ēgredī, ēgressus sum   *go out*
hortor, hortārī, hortātus sum   *encourage, urge*
ingredior, ingredī, ingressus sum   *enter*
loquor, loquī, locūtus sum   *speak*
morior, morī, mortuus sum   *die*
nāscor, nāscī, nātus sum   *be born*
patior, patī, passus sum   *suffer*
precor, precārī, precātus sum   *pray (to)*
proficīscor, proficīscī,
  profectus sum   *set out*
prōgredior, prōgredī,
  prōgressus sum   *advance*
regredior, regredī, regressus sum   *go back, return*
sequor, sequī, secūtus sum   *follow*
suspicor, suspicārī,
  suspicātus sum   *suspect*

An aureus of the Emperor Domitian.
Opposite: *An sestertius showing*
Domitia and her son.

LANGUAGE INFORMATION

Contents

Part One: About the language

Nouns

1

	first declension	*second declension*			*third declension*
GENDER	f.	m.	m.	n.	m.
SINGULAR					
nominative and vocative	puella	servus (*voc.* serve)	puer	templum	mercātor
accusative	puellam	servum	puerum	templum	mercātōrem
genitive (of)	puellae	servī	puerī	templī	mercātōris
dative (to, for)	puellae	servō	puerō	templō	mercātōrī
ablative (by, with)	puellā	servō	puerō	templō	mercātōre
PLURAL					
nominative and vocative	puellae	servī	puerī	templa	mercātōrēs
accusative	puellās	servōs	puerōs	templa	mercātōrēs
genitive (of)	puellārum	servōrum	puerōrum	templōrum	mercātōrum
dative (to, for)	puellīs	servīs	puerīs	templīs	mercātōribus
ablative (by, with)	puellīs	servīs	puerīs	templīs	mercātōribus

	fourth declension		*fifth declension*
GENDER	f.	n.	m.
SINGULAR			
nominative and vocative	manus	genū	diēs
accusative	manum	genū	diem
genitive (of)	manūs	genūs	diēī
dative (to, for)	manuī	genū	diēī
ablative (by, with)	manū	genū	diē
PLURAL			
nominative and vocative	manūs	genua	diēs
accusative	manūs	genua	diēs
genitive (of)	manuum	genuum	diērum
dative (to, for)	manibus	genibus	diēbus
ablative (by, with)	manibus	genibus	diēbus

m.	m.	m.	f.	n.	n.	GENDER
						SINGULAR
leō	cīvis	rēx	urbs	nōmen	tempus	*nominative and vocative*
leōnem	cīvem	rēgem	urbem	nōmen	tempus	*accusative*
leōnis	cīvis	rēgis	urbis	nōminis	temporis	*genitive (of)*
leōnī	cīvī	rēgī	urbī	nōminī	temporī	*dative (to, for)*
leōne	cīve	rēge	urbe	nōmine	tempore	*ablative (by, with)*
						PLURAL
leōnēs	cīvēs	rēgēs	urbēs	nōmina	tempora	*nominative and vocative*
leōnēs	cīvēs	rēgēs	urbēs	nōmina	tempora	*accusative*
leōnum	cīvium	rēgum	urbium	nōminum	temporum	*genitive (of)*
leōnibus	cīvibus	rēgibus	urbibus	nōminibus	temporibus	*dative (to, for)*
leōnibus	cīvibus	rēgibus	urbibus	nōminibus	temporibus	*ablative (by, with)*

2 For the ways in which the different cases are used, see p. 135.

3 Notice again the way in which the cases of third declension nouns are formed. In particular, compare the nominative singular of **leō**, **rēx** and **nōmen** with the genitive singular. Which of these cases is a better guide to the way the other cases are formed?

   Use the **Vocabulary** on pp. 143–59 to find the genitive singular of the following nouns; then use the tables here to find their ablative singular and plural:

   dux; homō; pēs; difficultās; nox; iter.

4 Translate the following pairs of sentences. State the case, number (i.e. singular or plural) and declension of each noun in **bold type**. Use the table of nouns to help you.

   a servī **nōmina** Graeca habēbant.
      fēmina pauper erat, sed vītam contentam agēbat.
   b magnus numerus **leōnum** in arēnam ruit.
      lībertus **coquum** iussit cēnam magnificam parāre.
   c **captīvī**, ē carcere ēductī, in pompā incedēbant.
      imperātor arcum **frātrī** dēdicāre cōnstituit.
   d **multitūdō** hominum viās urbis complēbat.
      puella, **ānulō** dēlectāta, iuvenī grātiās ēgit.

Adjectives

1 first and second declension

SINGULAR	masculine	feminine	neuter	masculine	feminine	neuter
nominative and vocative	bonus (voc. bone)	bona	bonum	pulcher	pulchra	pulchrum
accusative	bonum	bonam	bonum	pulchrum	pulchram	pulchrum
genitive	bonī	bonae	bonī	pulchrī	pulchrae	pulchrī
dative	bonō	bonae	bonō	pulchrō	pulchrae	pulchrō
ablative	bonō	bonā	bonō	pulchrō	pulchrā	pulchrō
PLURAL						
nominative and vocative	bonī	bonae	bona	pulchrī	pulchrae	pulchra
accusative	bonōs	bonās	bona	pulchrōs	pulchrās	pulchra
genitive	bonōrum	bonārum	bonōrum	pulchrōrum	pulchrārum	pulchrōrum
dative	bonīs	bonīs	bonīs	pulchrīs	pulchrīs	pulchrīs
ablative	bonīs	bonīs	bonīs	pulchrīs	pulchrīs	pulchrīs

2 third declension

SINGULAR	masculine and feminine	neuter	masculine and feminine	neuter
nominative and vocative	fortis	forte	ingēns	ingēns
accusative	fortem	forte	ingentem	ingēns
genitive	fortis	fortis	ingentis	ingentis
dative	fortī	fortī	ingentī	ingentī
ablative	fortī	fortī	ingentī	ingentī
PLURAL				
nominative and vocative	fortēs	fortia	ingentēs	ingentia
accusative	fortēs	fortia	ingentēs	ingentia
genitive	fortium	fortium	ingentium	ingentium
dative	fortibus	fortibus	ingentibus	ingentibus
ablative	fortibus	fortibus	ingentibus	ingentibus

3 Compare the third declension adjectives in paragraph 2 with the third declension nouns on pp. 114–15. Notice in particular the different form of the ablative singular.

4 With the help of paragraphs 1 and 2 opposite and the table of nouns on pp. 114–15, find the Latin for the words in *italic type* in the following sentences:

a I took the *brave girl* to the centurion.
b He was the son of a *good king*.
c They were attacked by a *huge slave*.
d We visited many *beautiful cities*.
e The walls of the *huge temples* were built slowly and carefully.
f The dancing-girl had *beautiful hands*.

5 Translate the following sentences. Then change the words in **bold type** into the plural. You may have to refer to the Vocabulary at the end of the book.

a pater **parvum fīlium** ad arcum Titī dūxit.
b senātor **fēminae trīstī** auxilium dedit.
c hostēs, **mūrō ingentī** dēfēnsī, diū resistēbant.
d omnēs audāciam **mīlitis Rōmānī** laudāvērunt.
e cīvēs **iuvenī callidō** praemium obtulērunt.
f **senex sapiēns** rēgī nōn **crēdidit**.

Comparatives and superlatives

1

	comparative	superlative
longus *long*	longior *longer*	longissimus *longest, very long*
pulcher *beautiful*	pulchrior *more beautiful*	pulcherrimus *most beautiful, very beautiful*
fortis *brave*	fortior *braver*	fortissimus *bravest, very brave*
fēlīx *lucky*	fēlīcior *luckier*	fēlīcissimus *luckiest, very lucky*
prūdēns *shrewd*	prūdentior *shrewder*	prūdentissimus *shrewdest, very shrewd*
facilis *easy*	facilior *easier*	facillimus *easiest, very easy*

2   Irregular forms

bonus *good*	melior *better*	optimus *best, very good*
malus *bad*	peior *worse*	pessimus *worst, very bad*
magnus *big*	maior *bigger*	maximus *biggest, very big*
parvus *small*	minor *smaller*	minimus *smallest, very small*
multus *much*	plūs *more*	plūrimus *most, very much*
multī *many*	plūrēs *more*	plūrimī *most, very many*

3 Study the forms of the comparative adjective **longior** (*longer*) and the superlative adjective **longissimus** (*longest, very long*):

SINGULAR	*masculine and feminine*	*neuter*	*masculine*	*feminine*	*neuter*
nominative and vocative	longior	longius	longissimus (*voc.* longissime)	longissima	longissimum
accusative	longiōrem	longius	longissimum	longissimam	longissimum
genitive	longiōris	longiōris	longissimī	longissimae	longissimī
dative	longiōrī	longiōrī	longissimō	longissimae	longissimō
ablative	longiōre	longiōre	longissimō	longissimā	longissimō
PLURAL					
nominative and vocative	longiōrēs	longiōra	longissimī	longissimae	longissima
accusative	longiōrēs	longiōra	longissimōs	longissimās	longissima
genitive	longiōrum	longiōrum	longissimōrum	longissimārum	longissimōrum
dative	longiōribus	longiōribus	longissimīs	longissimīs	longissimīs
ablative	longiōribus	longiōribus	longissimīs	longissimīs	longissimīs

4 Compare the endings of **longior** with those of the third declension nouns **mercātor** and **tempus** on pp. 114 and 115. Notice in particular the nominative and accusative forms of the neuter singular.

5 With the help of paragraphs 1–3 and the table of nouns on pp. 114–15, find the Latin for the words in *italic type* in the following sentences:

a I have never known a *longer day*.
b She sent the *worst slaves* back to the slave-dealer.
c *Better times* will come.
d The *bravest citizens* were fighting in the front line.
e We did not visit the *biggest temple*, as we had seen a *more beautiful temple* next to it.
f *Most girls* did not believe the soldiers' stories.

Pronouns I: **ego, tū, nōs, vōs, sē**

1 **ego** and **tū** (*I, you*, etc.)

	SINGULAR		PLURAL	
nominative	ego	tū	nōs	vōs
accusative	mē	tē	nōs	vōs
genitive	meī	tuī	nostrum	vestrum
dative	mihi	tibi	nōbīs	vōbīs
ablative	mē	tē	nōbīs	vōbīs

2 **sē** (*himself, herself, themselves*, etc.)

	SINGULAR	PLURAL
accusative	sē	sē
genitive	suī	suī
dative	sibi	sibi
ablative	sē	sē

3 Translate the following sentences:

a nōs, ā tē monitī, perīculum vītāvimus.
b captīvī, quod nūlla spēs salūtis erat, sē occīdērunt.
c vīsne mēcum īre?
d amīcī, quod diūtius manēre nōlēbant, domum sine vōbīs rediērunt.
e Salvius, cum ad aulam prōcēderet, multōs servōs sēcum habēbat.
f sorōrem rogāvī num stolās novās sibi comparāvisset.

Pick out the pronoun in each sentence and state its case.

Pronouns II: **hic, ille, ipse, is, īdem**

1 **hic** (*this*, *these*, etc.)

| | SINGULAR | | | PLURAL | | |
	masculine	*feminine*	*neuter*	*masculine*	*feminine*	*neuter*
nominative	hic	haec	hoc	hī	hae	haec
accusative	hunc	hanc	hoc	hōs	hās	haec
genitive	huius	huius	huius	hōrum	hārum	hōrum
dative	huic	huic	huic	hīs	hīs	hīs
ablative	hōc	hāc	hōc	hīs	hīs	hīs

The various forms of **hic** can also be used to mean *he, she, they*, etc.:

> hic tamen nihil dīcere poterat.
> *He, however, could say nothing.*

2 **ille** (*that*, *those*, etc.; sometimes used with the meaning *he, she, it*, etc.)

| | SINGULAR | | | PLURAL | | |
	masculine	*feminine*	*neuter*	*masculine*	*feminine*	*neuter*
nominative	ille	illa	illud	illī	illae	illa
accusative	illum	illam	illud	illōs	illās	illa
genitive	illīus	illīus	illīus	illōrum	illārum	illōrum
dative	illī	illī	illī	illīs	illīs	illīs
ablative	illō	illā	illō	illīs	illīs	illīs

3 **ipse** (*myself, yourself, himself*, etc.)

| | SINGULAR | | | PLURAL | | |
	masculine	*feminine*	*neuter*	*masculine*	*feminine*	*neuter*
nominative	ipse	ipsa	ipsum	ipsī	ipsae	ipsa
accusative	ipsum	ipsam	ipsum	ipsōs	ipsās	ipsa
genitive	ipsīus	ipsīus	ipsīus	ipsōrum	ipsārum	ipsōrum
dative	ipsī	ipsī	ipsī	ipsīs	ipsīs	ipsīs
ablative	ipsō	ipsā	ipsō	ipsīs	ipsīs	ipsīs

4 **is** (*he, she, it*, etc.)

	SINGULAR			PLURAL		
	masculine	*feminine*	*neuter*	*masculine*	*feminine*	*neuter*
nominative	is	ea	id	eī	eae	ea
accusative	eum	eam	id	eōs	eās	ea
genitive	eius	eius	eius	eōrum	eārum	eōrum
dative	eī	eī	eī	eīs	eīs	eīs
ablative	eō	eā	eō	eīs	eīs	eīs

The forms of **is** can also be used to mean *that, those*, etc.:

ĕā nocte rediit dominus.
That night, the master returned.

5 From Stage 23 onwards, you have met various forms of the word **īdem**, meaning *the same*:

	SINGULAR			PLURAL		
	masculine	*feminine*	*neuter*	*masculine*	*feminine*	*neuter*
nominative	īdem	eadem	idem	eīdem	eaedem	eadem
accusative	eundem	eandem	idem	eōsdem	eāsdem	eadem
genitive	eiusdem	eiusdem	eiusdem	eōrundem	eārundem	eōrundem
dative	eīdem	eīdem	eīdem	eīsdem	eīsdem	eīsdem
ablative	eōdem	eādem	eōdem	eīsdem	eīsdem	eīsdem

Compare the forms of **īdem** with **is** in paragraph 4.

With the help of the table above, find the Latin for the words in *italic type* in the following sentences:

a I heard *the same* boy again.
b *The same* women were there.
c This is *the same* man's house.
d He saw *the same* girl.
e They were seized by *the same* soldiers.
f They always visited *the same* temple.

Pronouns III: quī

1 Notice the genitive, dative and ablative plural of the relative pronoun **quī**:

	SINGULAR			PLURAL		
	masculine	*feminine*	*neuter*	*masculine*	*feminine*	*neuter*
nominative	quī	quae	quod	quī	quae	quae
accusative	quem	quam	quod	quōs	quās	quae
genitive	cuius	cuius	cuius	quōrum	quārum	quōrum
dative	cui	cui	cui	quibus	quibus	quibus
ablative	quō	quā	quō	quibus	quibus	quibus

duōs servōs ēmī, **quōrum** alter Graecus, alter Aegyptius erat.
*I bought two slaves, one **of whom** was a Greek, the other an Egyptian.*

nūntiī, **quibus** mandāta dedimus heri discessērunt.
*The messengers **to whom** we gave the instructions departed yesterday.*

mīlitēs aedificia, **ē quibus** hostēs fūgerant, celeriter incendērunt.
*The soldiers quickly set fire to the buildings, **from which** the enemy had fled.*

2 Notice again the use of **quī** as a *connecting relative* to begin a sentence:

lībertus pecūniam custōdiēbat. **quem** cum cōnspexissent, fūrēs fūgērunt.
*A freedman was guarding the money. When they had caught sight **of him** the thieves ran away.*

centuriō 'ad carnificēs dūcite!' inquit. **quibus** verbīs perterritī, captīvī clāmāre ac lacrimāre coepērunt.
*'Take them to the executioners!' said the centurion. Terrified **by these** words, the prisoners began to shout and weep.*

3 Sometimes the relative pronoun is used with forms of the pronoun **is**:

fēcī **id quod** iussistī.
*I have done **that which** you ordered.*

Or, in more natural English, using the word *what* to translate both Latin words:

fēcī **id quod** iussistī.
*I have done **what** you ordered.*

Further examples:

a id quod Salvius in epistulā scrīpsit falsum est.
b id quod mihi dīxistī vix intellegere possum.
c nūntius ea patefēcit quae apud Britannōs audīverat.
d servus tamen, homō ignāvissimus, id quod dominus iusserat omnīnō neglēxit.
e ea quae fēcistī ab omnibus laudantur.

Verbs

Indicative active

1

		first conjugation	second conjugation	third conjugation	fourth conjugation
PRESENT		*I carry, you carry, etc.*	*I teach, you teach, etc.*	*I drag, you drag, etc.*	*I hear, you hear, etc.*
		portō	doceō	trahō	audiō
		portās	docēs	trahis	audīs
		portat	docet	trahit	audit
		portāmus	docēmus	trahimus	audīmus
		portātis	docētis	trahitis	audītis
		portant	docent	trahunt	audiunt
IMPERFECT		*I was carrying*	*I was teaching*	*I was dragging*	*I was hearing*
		portābam	docēbam	trahēbam	audiēbam
		portābās	docēbās	trahēbās	audiēbās
		portābat	docēbat	trahēbat	audiēbat
		portābāmus	docēbāmus	trahēbāmus	audiēbāmus
		portābātis	docēbātis	trahēbātis	audiēbātis
		portābant	docēbant	trahēbant	audiēbant

2   In Stage 33, you met the *future tense*:

I shall carry	*I shall teach*	*I shall drag*	*I shall hear*
portābō	docēbō	traham	audiam
portābis	docēbis	trahēs	audiēs
portābit	docēbit	trahet	audiet
portābimus	docēbimus	trahēmus	audiēmus
portābitis	docēbitis	trahētis	audiētis
portābunt	docēbunt	trahent	audient

Notice again how the first and second conjugations form their future tense in one way, the third and fourth conjugations in another.

3   In paragraph 2, find the Latin for:

they will carry; we shall drag; you (s.) will teach; I shall hear; you (pl.) will drag; he will carry.

4 Translate the following examples:

audiēmus; portābit; mittent; aedificābitis; veniam; manēbis.

5 Translate each verb in the list below. Then with the help of paragraph 2 change it into the future tense, keeping the same person and number (i.e. 1st person singular, etc.). Then translate again.

For example: **portāmus** (*we carry*) would become **portābimus** (*we shall carry*).

portātis; docēbam; docēbāmus; trahō; audīs; audiēbat.

6

	first conjugation	second conjugation	third conjugation	fourth conjugation
PERFECT	*I (have) carried*	*I (have) taught*	*I (have) dragged*	*I (have) heard*
	portāvī	docuī	trāxī	audīvī
	portāvistī	docuistī	trāxistī	audīvistī
	portāvit	docuit	trāxit	audīvit
	portāvimus	docuimus	trāximus	audīvimus
	portāvistis	docuistis	trāxistis	audīvistis
	portāvērunt	docuērunt	trāxērunt	audīvērunt
PLUPERFECT	*I had carried*	*I had taught*	*I had dragged*	*I had heard*
	portāveram	docueram	trāxeram	audīveram
	portāverās	docuerās	trāxerās	audīverās
	portāverat	docuerat	trāxerat	audīverat
	portāverāmus	docuerāmus	trāxerāmus	audīverāmus
	portāverātis	docuerātis	trāxerātis	audīverātis
	portāverant	docuerant	trāxerant	audīverant

7 In Stage 33, you met the *future perfect tense*:

I shall have carried	*I shall have taught*	*I shall have dragged*	*I shall have heard*
portāverō	docuerō	trāxerō	audīverō
portāveris	docueris	trāxeris	audīveris
portāverit	docuerit	trāxerit	audīverit
portāverimus	docuerimus	trāxerimus	audīverimus
portāveritis	docueritis	trāxeritis	audīveritis
portāverint	docuerint	trāxerint	audīverint

The future perfect is often translated by an English present tense:

sī effūgerō, iter ad vōs faciam.
If I escape, I shall make my way to you.

Indicative passive

1 In Stage 29, you met the following forms of the *passive*:

	first conjugation	*second conjugation*	*third conjugation*	*fourth conjugation*
PRESENT	portātur *s/he is (being) carried*	docētur *s/he is (being) taught*	trahitur *s/he is (being) dragged*	audītur *s/he is (being) heard*
	portantur *they are (being) carried*	docentur *they are (being) taught*	trahuntur *they are (being) dragged*	audiuntur *they are (being) heard*
IMPERFECT	portābātur *s/he was being carried*	docēbātur *s/he was being taught*	trahēbātur *s/he was being dragged*	audiēbātur *s/he was being heard*
	portābantur *they were being carried*	docēbantur *they were being taught*	trahēbantur *they were being dragged*	audiēbantur *they were being heard*

2 Translate each verb, then change it from singular to plural, so that it means *they …* instead of *s/he* or *it …* . Then translate again.

   audītur; trahēbātur; dūcēbātur; laudātur; custōdiēbātur; dēlētur

3 In Stage 34 you met the *future tense* of the *passive*:

portābitur *s/he will be carried*	docēbitur *s/he will be taught*	trahētur *s/he will be dragged*	audiētur *s/he will be heard*
portābuntur *they will be carried*	docēbuntur *they will be taught*	trahentur *they will be dragged*	audientur *they will be heard*

4 The present, imperfect and future tenses above are shown only in the forms of the 3rd person singular and plural. You have not yet met the 1st and 2nd persons (*I am carried, you are carried*, etc.).

5 In Stage 30, you met the *perfect* and *pluperfect tenses* of the passive:

	first conjugation	*second conjugation*	*third conjugation*	*fourth conjugation*
PERFECT	*I have been carried, I was carried*	*I have been taught, I was taught*	*I have been dragged, I was dragged*	*I have been heard, I was heard*
	portātus sum	doctus sum	tractus sum	audītus sum
	portātus es	doctus es	tractus es	audītus es
	portātus est	doctus est	tractus est	audītus est
	portātī sumus	doctī sumus	tractī sumus	audītī sumus
	portātī estis	doctī estis	tractī estis	audītī estis
	portātī sunt	doctī sunt	tractī sunt	audītī sunt
PLUPERFECT	*I had been carried*	*I had been taught*	*I had been dragged*	*I had been heard*
	portātus eram	doctus eram	tractus eram	audītus eram
	portātus erās	doctus erās	tractus erās	audītus erās
	portātus erat	doctus erat	tractus erat	audītus erat
	portātī erāmus	doctī erāmus	tractī erāmus	audītī erāmus
	portātī erātis	doctī erātis	tractī erātis	audītī erātis
	portātī erant	doctī erant	tractī erant	audītī erant

6 Give the meaning of:

audītus eram; portātus erat; portātī sunt; doctus sum; tractus es; portātī erāmus.

7 In paragraph 5, find the Latin for:

they had been carried; I have been dragged; you (s.) have been taught; he was carried.

8 Notice again that the two tenses in paragraph 5 are formed with perfect passive participles, which change their endings to indicate *gender* (masculine, feminine and neuter) and *number* (singular and plural). For example:

masculine singular	puer ā mīlitibus **captus** est.
neuter singular	templum ā mīlitibus **captum** est.
feminine singular	urbs ā mīlitibus **capta** est.
feminine plural	multae urbēs ā mīlitibus **captae** sunt.

9 Translate the following examples:

docta est; tractum erat; vocātus sum; custōdītae sunt; missī erāmus; monita erās; ductī sunt; dēlēta sunt.

Subjunctive

1

	first conjugation	*second conjugation*	*third conjugation*	*fourth conjugation*
IMPERFECT SUBJUNCTIVE	portārem	docērem	traherem	audīrem
	portārēs	docērēs	traherēs	audīrēs
	portāret	docēret	traheret	audīret
	portārēmus	docērēmus	traherēmus	audīrēmus
	portārētis	docērētis	traherētis	audīrētis
	portārent	docērent	traherent	audīrent
PLUPERFECT SUBJUNCTIVE	portāvissem	docuissem	trāxissem	audīvissem
	portāvissēs	docuissēs	trāxissēs	audīvissēs
	portāvisset	docuisset	trāxisset	audīvisset
	portāvissēmus	docuissēmus	trāxissēmus	audīvissēmus
	portāvissētis	docuissētis	trāxissētis	audīvissētis
	portāvissent	docuissent	trāxissent	audīvissent

2   For ways in which the subjunctive is used see pp. 138–9.

Other forms of the verb

1

	to carry	*to teach*	*to drag*	*to hear*
PRESENT ACTIVE INFINITIVE	portāre	docēre	trahere	audīre

2

	to be carried	*to be taught*	*to be dragged*	*to be heard*
PRESENT PASSIVE INFINITIVE	portārī	docērī	trahī	audīrī

3

	carry!	*teach!*	*drag!*	*hear!*
IMPERATIVE SINGULAR	portā	docē	trahe	audī
PLURAL	portāte	docēte	trahite	audīte

4

PRESENT PARTICIPLE	*carrying* portāns	*teaching* docēns	*dragging* trahēns	*hearing* audiēns

Study the forms of the present participle **portāns**:

	SINGULAR *masculine and feminine*	*neuter*	PLURAL *masculine and feminine*	*neuter*
nominative and vocative	portāns	portāns	portantēs	portantia
accusative	portantem	portāns	portantēs	portantia
genitive	portantis	portantis	portantium	portantium
dative	portantī	portantī	portantibus	portantibus
ablative	portantī	portantī	portantibus	portantibus

The ablative singular of present participles sometimes ends in **-e**, e.g. **portante**, **docente**.

5

PERFECT PASSIVE PARTICIPLE	*(having been) carried* portātus	*(having been) taught* doctus	*(having been) dragged* tractus	*(having been) heard* audītus

Perfect passive participles change their endings in the same way as **bonus** (shown on p. 116).

For examples of perfect *active* participles, see **Deponent verbs**, p. 130.

6

FUTURE PARTICIPLE	*about to carry* portātūrus	*about to teach* doctūrus	*about to drag* tractūrus	*about to hear* audītūrus

Future participles change their endings in the same way as **bonus**.

For examples of ways in which participles are used, see pp. 136–7.

7

GERUNDIVE	portandus	docendus	trahendus	audiendus

Gerundives change their endings in the same way as **bonus**.

Notice again the way in which the gerundive is used:

nōbīs audiendum est.   mihi amphora portanda est.
We must listen.   *I must carry the wine-jar.*

Deponent verbs

1. From Stage 32 onwards, you have met *deponent verbs*:

PRESENT	cōnātur	*s/he tries*	loquitur	*s/he speaks*
	cōnantur	*they try*	loquuntur	*they speak*
IMPERFECT	cōnābātur	*s/he was trying*	loquēbātur	*s/he was speaking*
	cōnābantur	*they were trying*	loquēbantur	*they were speaking*
PERFECT	cōnātus sum	*I (have) tried*	locūtus sum	*I spoke, I have spoken*
	cōnātus es	*you (have) tried*	locūtus es	*you spoke, you have spoken*
	cōnātus est	*he (has) tried*	locūtus est	*he spoke, he has spoken*
	cōnātī sumus	*we (have) tried*	locūtī sumus	*we spoke, we have spoken*
	cōnātī estis	*you (have) tried*	locūtī estis	*you spoke, you have spoken*
	cōnātī sunt	*they (have) tried*	locūtī sunt	*they spoke, they have spoken*
PLUPERFECT	cōnātus eram	*I had tried*	locūtus eram	*I had spoken*
	cōnātus erās	*you had tried*	locūtus erās	*you had spoken*
	cōnātus erat	*he had tried*	locūtus erat	*he had spoken*
	cōnātī erāmus	*we had tried*	locūtī erāmus	*we had spoken*
	cōnātī erātis	*you had tried*	locūtī erātis	*you had spoken*
	cōnātī erant	*they had tried*	locūtī erant	*they had spoken*
PERFECT ACTIVE PARTICIPLE	cōnātus	*having tried*	locūtus	*having spoken*

Perfect active participles change their endings in the same way as **bonus** (shown on p. 116).

PRESENT INFINITIVE	cōnārī	*to try*	loquī	*to speak*

2. In Stage 34 you met the *future tense* of deponent verbs:

	cōnābitur	*s/he will try*	loquētur	*s/he will speak*
	cōnābuntur	*they will try*	loquentur	*they will speak*

3. The present, imperfect and future tenses above are shown only in the form of the 3rd person singular and plural. You have not yet met the 1st and 2nd persons (*I try, you try*, etc.) in the stories in the Stages.

4 Give the meaning of:

cōnātus eram; locūtī sumus; ingressī sumus; ingressus erās; profectus es; profectī erāmus; secūtī sunt; hortātī erātis.

5 Translate each word (or pair of words), then change it from plural to singular, so that it means *he ...* instead of *they ...* . Then translate again.

loquuntur; cōnātī sunt; profectī sunt; hortantur; sequēbantur; ēgressī erant; precābuntur; loquentur.

6 Compare the two verbs in paragraphs 1 and 2 with the passive forms of **portō** and **trahō** listed on pp. 126–7 above.

7 For further practice of deponent verbs, see paragraphs 4–5 on p. 142.

Irregular verbs

Indicative

1

PRESENT	*I am*	*I am able*	*I go*	*I want*	*I bring*	*I take*
	sum	possum	eō	volō	ferō	capiō
	es	potes	īs	vīs	fers	capis
	est	potest	it	vult	fert	capit
	sumus	possumus	īmus	volumus	ferimus	capimus
	estis	potestis	ītis	vultis	fertis	capitis
	sunt	possunt	eunt	volunt	ferunt	capiunt

IMPERFECT	*I was*	*I was able*	*I was going*	*I was wanting*	*I was bringing*	*I was taking*
	eram	poteram	ībam	volēbam	ferēbam	capiēbam
	erās	poterās	ībās	volēbās	ferēbās	capiēbās
	erat	poterat	ībat	volēbat	ferēbat	capiēbat
	erāmus	poterāmus	ībāmus	volēbāmus	ferēbāmus	capiēbāmus
	erātis	poterātis	ībātis	volēbātis	ferēbātis	capiēbātis
	erant	poterant	ībant	volēbant	ferēbant	capiēbant

2 Study the forms of the *future tense*:

I shall be	*I shall be able*	*I shall go*	*I shall want*	*I shall bring*	*I shall take*
erō	poterō	ībō	volam	feram	capiam
eris	poteris	ībis	volēs	ferēs	capiēs
erit	poterit	ībit	volet	feret	capiet
erimus	poterimus	ībimus	volēmus	ferēmus	capiēmus
eritis	poteritis	ībitis	volētis	ferētis	capiētis
erunt	poterunt	ībunt	volent	ferent	capient

3 Translate each verb, then change it into the future tense, keeping the same person and number (i.e. 1st person singular, etc.). Then translate again.

    est; potestis; ībam; vīs; ferunt; capiēbāmus.

4						
PERFECT	*I have been,* *I was* fuī fuistī fuit fuimus fuistis fuērunt	*I have been able, I was able* potuī potuistī potuit potuimus potuistis potuērunt	*I have gone,* *I went* iī iistī iit iimus iistis iērunt	*I (have) wanted* voluī voluistī voluit voluimus voluistis voluērunt	*I (have) brought* tulī tulistī tulit tulimus tulistis tulērunt	*I have taken,* *I took* cēpī cēpistī cēpit cēpimus cēpistis cēpērunt
PLUPERFECT	*I had been* fueram fuerās fuerat fuerāmus fuerātis fuerant	*I had been able* potueram potuerās potuerat potuerāmus potuerātis potuerant	*I had gone* ieram ierās ierat ierāmus ierātis ierant	*I had wanted* volueram voluerās voluerat voluerāmus voluerātis voluerant	*I had brought* tuleram tulerās tulerat tulerāmus tulerātis tulerant	*I had taken* cēperam cēperās cēperat cēperāmus cēperātis cēperant

5   Study the following *passive* forms of **ferō** and **capiō**:

PRESENT	fertur feruntur	*s/he is brought* *they are brought*	capitur capiuntur	*s/he is taken* *they are taken*
IMPERFECT	ferēbātur ferēbantur	*s/he was being brought* *they were being brought*	capiēbātur capiēbantur	*s/he was being taken* *they were being taken*
FUTURE	ferētur ferentur	*s/he will be brought* *they will be brought*	capiētur capientur	*s/he will be taken* *they will be taken*
PERFECT	lātus sum lātus es etc.	*I have been brought,* *I was brought* *you have been brought,* *you were brought*	captus sum captus es etc.	*I have been taken,* *I was taken* *you have been taken,* *you were taken*
PLUPERFECT	lātus eram lātus erās etc.	*I had been brought* *you had been brought*	captus eram captus erās etc.	*I had been taken* *you had been taken*
PERFECT PASSIVE PARTICIPLE	lātus	*having been brought*	captus	*having been taken*

6   Give the meaning of:

       captus erat; lātī erant; lātī sunt; captī sumus.

     What would be the Latin for the following:

       he had been brought; he has been taken; we have been brought; they were taken.

Subjunctive

IMPERFECT SUBJUNCTIVE	essem	possem	īrem	vellem	ferrem	caperem
	essēs	possēs	īrēs	vellēs	ferrēs	caperēs
	esset	posset	īret	vellet	ferret	caperet
	essēmus	possēmus	īrēmus	vellēmus	ferrēmus	caperēmus
	essētis	possētis	īrētis	vellētis	ferrētis	caperētis
	essent	possent	īrent	vellent	ferrent	caperent
PLUPERFECT SUBJUNCTIVE	fuissem	potuissem	iissem	voluissem	tulissem	cēpissem
	fuissēs	potuissēs	iissēs	voluissēs	tulissēs	cēpissēs
	fuisset	potuisset	iisset	voluisset	tulisset	cēpisset
	fuissēmus	potuissēmus	iissēmus	voluissēmus	tulissēmus	cēpissēmus
	fuissētis	potuissētis	iissētis	voluissētis	tulissētis	cēpissētis
	fuissent	potuissent	iissent	voluissent	tulissent	cēpissent

Other forms of the verb

PRESENT INFINITIVE	esse *to be*	posse *to be able*	īre *to go*	velle *to want*	ferre *to bring*	capere *to take*

Uses of the cases

1 *nominative*
    captīvus clāmābat.   *The prisoner was shouting.*

2 *vocative*
    valē, **domine**!   *Goodbye, master!*

3 *accusative*
  a **pontem** trānsiimus.   *We crossed the bridge.*
  b **trēs hōrās** labōrābam.   *I was working for three hours.*
  c per **agrōs**; ad **vīllam**   *through the fields; to the house*
  d in **forum**   *into the forum*

4 *genitive*
  a māter **puerōrum**   *the mother of the boys*
  b plūs **pecūniae**   *more money*
  c vir **maximae virtūtis**   *a man of very great courage*

5 *dative*
  a **mīlitibus** cibum dedimus.   *We gave food to the soldiers.*
  b **vestrō candidātō** nōn faveō.   *I do not support your candidate.*

6 *ablative*
  a **spectāculō** attonitus   *astonished by the sight*
  b senex **longā barbā**   *an old man with a long beard*
  c **nōbilī gente** nātus   *born from a noble family*
  d **quārtō diē** revēnit.   *He came back on the fourth day.*
  e cum **amīcīs**; ab **urbe**; in **forō**   *with friends; away from the city; in the forum*

For examples of ablative absolute phrases, see paragraph 4 on p. 136.

7 Further examples of some of the uses listed above:

  a Salvius erat vir summae calliditātis.
  b decimā hōrā ex oppidō contendimus.
  c uxor imperātōris, in ātrium ingressa, ancillīs fidēlibus grātiās ēgit.
  d fabrī, spē praemiī incitātī, arcum ante prīmam lūcem perfēcērunt.
  e multōs diēs Haterius ē vīllā discēdere recūsāvit.
  f Salvī, cūr cōnsiliīs meīs obstās?
  g senātor in lectō manēbat quod nimium cibī cōnsūmpserat.
  h lēgātus mīlitibus imperāvit ut hostēs hastīs gladiīsque oppugnārent.

Uses of the participle

1 In Book III you saw how a participle changes its endings to agree with the noun it describes.

2 Notice again some of the various ways in which a participle can be translated:

> fūrēs, canem cōnspicātī, fūgērunt.
> *The thieves, having caught sight of the dog, ran away.*
> *When the thieves caught sight of the dog, they ran away.*
> *On catching sight of the dog, the thieves ran away.*
> *The thieves ran away because they had caught sight of the dog.*

3 Translate the following examples:

> **a** ingēns multitūdō pompam per Viam Sacram prōcēdentem spectābat.
> **b** custōdēs puerō lacrimantī nihil dīxērunt.
> **c** mīlitēs, ā centuriōnibus iussī, in longīs ōrdinibus stābant.
> **d** mercātor amīcōs, ā Graeciā regressōs, ad cēnam sūmptuōsam invītāvit.

Pick out the noun and participle pair in each sentence, and say whether it is nominative, accusative or dative, singular or plural.

4 In Stage 31, you met examples of *ablative absolute* phrases, consisting of a noun and participle in the ablative case:

> bellō cōnfectō, Agricola ad Ītaliam rediit.
> *With the war having been finished, Agricola returned to Italy.*

Or, in more natural English:
> *When the war had been finished, Agricola returned to Italy*, or,
> *After finishing the war, Agricola returned to Italy.*

Further examples:

> **a** ponte dēlētō, nēmō flūmen trānsīre poterat.
> **b** hīs verbīs audītīs, cīvēs plausērunt.
> **c** nāve refectā, mercātor ā Britanniā discessit.
> **d** iuvenēs, togīs dēpositīs, balneum intrāvērunt.
> **e** latrōnēs, omnibus dormientibus, tabernam incendērunt.
> **f** cōnsule ingressō, omnēs senātōrēs surrēxērunt.
> **g** fēle absente, mūrēs lūdere solent.

5 From Stage 31 onwards, you have met examples in which a noun and participle in the *dative* case are placed at the beginning of the sentence:

> **amīcō** auxilium **petentī** multam pecūniam obtulī.
> ***To a friend asking for*** *help I offered a lot of money.*

Or, in more natural English:
> *When my friend asked for help I offered him a lot of money.*

Further examples:

a servō haesitantī Vitellia 'intra!' inquit.
b Hateriō haec rogantī Salvius nihil respondit.
c praecōnī regressō senex epistulam trādidit.
d puellae prōcēdentī obstābat ingēns multitūdō clientium.

Uses of the subjunctive

1   with **cum** (meaning *when*)

> Iūdaeī, cum cōnsilium Eleazārī audīvissent, libenter cōnsēnsērunt.
> *When the Jews had heard Eleazar's plan, they willingly agreed.*

2   *indirect question*

> cōnsul nesciēbat quis arcum novum aedificāvisset.
> *The consul did not know who had built the new arch.*

> mē rogāvērunt num satis pecūniae habērem.
> *They asked me whether I had enough money.*

From Stage 28 onwards, you have met the words **utrum** and **an** in indirect questions:

> incertī erant utrum dux mortuus an vīvus esset.
> *They were unsure whether their leader was dead or alive.*

3   *purpose clause*

> ad urbem iter fēcimus ut amphitheātrum vīsitārēmus.
> *We travelled to the city in order to visit the amphitheatre.*

In Stage 29, you met purpose clauses used with the relative pronoun **quī**:

> nūntiōs ēmīsit quī prīncipēs ad aulam arcesserent.
> *He sent out messengers who were to summon the chieftains to the palace.*

Or, in more natural English:
> *He sent out messengers to summon the chieftains to the palace.*

From Stage 29 onwards, you have met purpose clauses used with **nē**:

> centuriō omnēs portās clausit nē captīvī effugerent.
> *The centurion shut all the gates so that the prisoners should not escape.*

4   *indirect command*

> Domitiānus Salviō imperāverat ut rēgnum Cogidubnī occupāret.
> *Domitian had ordered Salvius to seize Cogidubnus' kingdom.*

From Stage 29 onwards, you have met indirect commands introduced by **nē**:

> puella agricolam ōrāvit nē equum occīderet.
> *The girl begged the farmer not to kill the horse.*

> Haterius ab amīcīs monitus est nē Salviō cōnfīderet.
> *Haterius was warned by friends not to trust Salvius.*

5 *result clause*

> tam perītus erat faber ut omnēs eum laudārent.
> *The craftsman was so skilful that everyone praised him.*

6 Translate the following examples:

    a cīvēs Rōmānī templa vīsitābant ut dīs grātiās agerent.
    b cum servī vīnum intulissent, Haterius silentium poposcit.
    c tanta erat fortitūdō Iūdaeōrum ut perīre potius quam cēdere māllent.
    d nēmō sciēbat utrum Haterius an Salvius rem administrāvisset.
    e uxor mihi persuāsit nē hoc susciperem.
    f extrā carcerem stābant decem mīlitēs quī captīvōs custōdīrent.

In each sentence, give the reason why a subjunctive is being used.

7 From Stage 33 onwards, you have met the subjunctive used with **priusquam** (meaning *before*) and **dum** (meaning *until*):

> Myropnous iānuam clausit priusquam mīlitēs intrārent.
> *Myropnous shut the door before the soldiers could enter.*

> exspectābam dum amīcus advenīret.
> *I was waiting until my friend should arrive.*

Or, in more natural English:
> *I was waiting for my friend to arrive.*

Longer sentences

1   Study each sentence and answer the questions that follow it:

   a   postquam Haterius fabrōs, quī labōrābant in āreā, dīmīsit, Salvius
       negōtium agere coepit.
       Where were the craftsmen working? What did Haterius do to them? What did
       Salvius then do?
       Now translate the sentence.

   b   spectātōrēs, cum candēlābrum aureum ē templō Iūdaeōrum raptum
       cōnspexissent, iterum iterumque plausērunt.
       What did the spectators catch sight of? From where had it been seized? What
       was the reaction of the spectators?
       Now translate the sentence.

   c   fūr, cum verba centuriōnis audīvisset, tantō metū poenārum affectus
       est ut pecūniam quam ē tabernā abstulerat, statim abicere cōnstitueret.
       What did the thief hear? How was he affected? What did he decide to do?
       Where had the money come from?
       Now translate the sentence.

2   Further examples for study and translation:

   a   ancillae, quod dominam vehementer clāmantem audīvērunt,
       cubiculum eius quam celerrimē petīvērunt.

   b   equitēs adeō pugnāre cupiēbant ut, simulac dux signum dedit, ē portīs
       castrōrum ērumperent.

   c   postquam cōnsul hanc sententiam dīxit, Domitiānus servō adstantī
       imperāvit ut epistulam ab Agricolā nūper missam recitāret.

   d   cum Haterius sōlus domī manēret, Vitellia eum anxia rogāvit cūr
       amīcōs clientēsque admittere nōllet.

   e   quamquam fēminae Simōnem frātrēsque cēlāvērunt nē perīrent,
       Rōmānī eōs comprehēnsōs ad Ītaliam mīsērunt.

Numerals

I	ūnus	1	XVI	sēdecim	16
II	duo	2	XVII	septendecim	17
III	trēs	3	XVIII	duodēvīgintī	18
IV	quattuor	4	XIX	ūndēvīgintī	19
V	quīnque	5	XX	vīgintī	20
VI	sex	6	XXX	trīgintā	30
VII	septem	7	XL	quadrāgintā	40
VIII	octō	8	L	quīnquāgintā	50
IX	novem	9	LX	sexāgintā	60
X	decem	10	LXX	septuāgintā	70
XI	ūndecim	11	LXXX	octōgintā	80
XII	duodecim	12	XC	nōnāgintā	90
XIII	trēdecim	13	C	centum	100
XIV	quattuordecim	14	M	mīlle	1000
XV	quīndecim	15	MM	duo mīlia	2000

Part Two: Vocabulary

Notes

1   Nouns, adjectives and most verbs are listed as in the Book III Language Information section.

2   Prepositions used with the ablative, such as **ex**, are marked + *abl.*; those used with the accusative, such as **per**, are marked + *acc.*

3   Deponent verbs (met and explained in Stage 32) are listed in the following way:

> The 1st person singular of the present tense. This always ends in **-or**, e.g. **cōnor** (*I try*).
> The infinitive. This always ends in **-ī**, e.g. **cōnārī** (*to try*).
> The 1st person singular of the perfect tense, e.g. **cōnātus sum** (*I tried*).
> The meaning.

So if the following forms are given:

> loquor, loquī, locūtus sum   *speak*

loquor means *I speak*, **loquī** means *to speak*, **locūtus sum** means *I spoke*.

4   Study the following deponent verbs, listed in the way described in paragraph 3.

> cōnspicor, cōnspicārī, cōnspicātus sum   *catch sight of*
> ingredior, ingredī, ingressus sum   *enter*
> lābor, lābī, lāpsus sum   *fall*

Give the meaning of:

> cōnspicor, ingredī, lāpsus sum, ingredior, cōnspicātus sum, lābī.

5   Use the **Vocabulary** on pp. 143–59 to find the meaning of:

> ēgredior, hortātus sum, pollicērī, sequor, minārī, adeptus sum.

6   All words which are given in the **Vocabulary checklists** for Stages 1–34 are marked with an asterisk(*).

a

*ā, ab + *abl.*   *from; by*
abdūcō, abdūcere, abdūxī,
   abductus   *lead away*
*abeō, abīre, abiī   *go away*
abhinc   *ago*
abhorreō, abhorrēre,
   abhorruī   *shrink (from)*
abigō, abigere, abēgī, abāctus   *drive away*
ablātus *see* auferre
absēns, *gen.* absentis   *absent*
absentia, absentiae, f.   *absence*
*absum, abesse, āfuī   *be out, be absent, be away*
*ac   *and*
*accidō, accidere, accidī   *happen*
*accipiō, accipere, accēpī,
   acceptus   *accept, take in, receive*
*accūsō, accūsāre, accūsāvī,
   accūsātus   *accuse*
āctor, āctōris, m.   *actor*
āctus *see* agō
*ad + *acc.*   *to, at*
addō, addere, addidī,
   additus   *add*
*adeō   *so much, so greatly*
*adeō, adīre, adiī   *approach, go up to*
adeptus *see* adipīscor
adest *see* adsum
*adhūc   *up till now*
*adipīscor, adipīscī,
   adeptus sum   *receive, obtain*
*adiuvō, adiuvāre, adiūvī   *help*
adligō, adligāre, adligāvī,
   adligātus   *tie*
adloquor, adloquī,
   adlocūtus sum   *speak to, address*
administrō, administrāre,
   administrāvī,
   administrātus   *look after, manage*
admīrātiō, admīrātiōnis, f.   *admiration*
admīror, admīrārī,
   admīrātus sum   *admire*
admittō, admittere, admīsī,
   admissus   *admit, let in*
adōrō, adōrāre, adōrāvī,
   adōrātus   *worship*
adstō, adstāre, adstitī   *stand by*
*adsum, adesse, adfuī   *be here, be present*
*adveniō, advenīre, advēnī   *arrive*
adventus, adventūs, m.   *arrival*
*adversus, adversa, adversum   *hostile, unfavourable*
*   rēs adversae   *misfortune*
*aedificium, aedificiī, n.   *building*
*aedificō, aedificāre,
   aedificāvī, aedificātus   *build*
*aeger, aegra, aegrum   *sick, ill*
aegrōtus, aegrōtī, m.   *invalid*

Aegyptius, Aegyptia,
   Aegyptium   *Egyptian*
Aegyptus, Aegyptī, f.   *Egypt*
*aequus, aequa, aequum   *fair, calm*
   aequō animō   *calmly, with a calm mind*
aeternus, aeterna, aeternum   *eternal*
Aethiopes, Aethiopum, m.pl.   *Ethiopians*
*afficiō, afficere, affēcī,
   affectus   *affect*
*   affectus, affecta, affectum   *affected, overcome*
afflīgō, afflīgere, afflīxī,
   afflīctus   *afflict, hurt*
agellus, agellī, m.   *small plot of land*
ager, agrī, m.   *field*
agger, aggeris, m.   *ramp, mound*
*agitō, agitāre, agitāvī, agitātus *chase, hunt*
*agmen, agminis, n.   *column (of men), procession*
*agnōscō, agnōscere, agnōvī,
   agnitus   *recognise*
*agō, agere, ēgī, āctus   *do, act*
   age!   *come on!*
   fābulam agere   *act a play*
*   grātiās agere   *thank, give thanks*
   negōtium agere   *do business, work*
   vītam agere   *lead a life*
*agricola, agricolae, m.   *farmer*
aliquandō   *sometimes*
*aliquis, aliquid   *someone, something*
   aliquid mīrī   *something extraordinary*
*alius, alia, aliud   *other, another, else*
*   aliī … aliī   *some … others*
*alter, altera, alterum   *the other, the second*
   alter … alter   *one … the other*
*altus, alta, altum   *high, deep*
ambitiō, ambitiōnis, f.   *bribery*
*ambō, ambae, ambō   *both*
*ambulō, ambulāre, ambulāvī   *walk*
āmēns, *gen.* āmentis   *out of one's mind, in a frenzy*
*amīcus, amīcī, m.   *friend*
*āmittō, āmittere, āmīsī,
   āmissus   *lose*
*amō, amāre, amāvī, amātus   *love, like* .
*amor, amōris, m.   *love*
amphitheātrum,
   amphitheātrī, n.   *amphitheatre*
amphora, amphorae, f.   *wine-jar*
amplector, amplectī,
   amplexus sum   *embrace*
amplissimus, amplissima,
   amplissimum   *very great*
amputō, amputāre, amputāvī,
   amputātus   *cut off*
an   *or*
*ancilla, ancillae, f.   *slave-girl, maid*
angelus, angelī, m.   *angel*
angustus, angusta, angustum   *narrow*
*animus, animī, m.   *spirit, soul, mind*
   aequō animō   *calmly, with a calm mind*
   in animō volvere   *wonder, turn over in the
                                        mind*

*annus, annī, m.	year
*ante + *acc.*	before, in front of
*anteā	before
*ānulus, ānulī, m.	ring
anus, anūs, f.	old woman
anxius, anxia, anxium	anxious
aper, aprī, m.	boar
*aperiō, aperīre, aperuī, apertus	open
apertē	openly
*appāreō, appārēre, appāruī	appear
*appellō, appellāre, appellāvī, appellātus	call, call out to
*appropinquō, appropinquāre, appropinquāvī	approach, come near to
aptus, apta, aptum	suitable
*apud + *acc.*	among, at the house of
*aqua, aquae, f.	water
*āra, ārae, f.	altar
arbiter, arbitrī, m.	expert, judge
arbor, arboris, f.	tree
*arcessō, arcessere, arcessīvī, arcessītus	summon, send for
architectus, architectī, m.	builder, architect
arcus, arcūs, m.	arch
*ardeō, ardēre, arsī	burn, be on fire
ardor, ardōris, m.	spirit, enthusiasm
ārea, āreae, f.	courtyard, builder's yard
arēna, arēnae, f.	arena
argenteus, argentea, argenteum	made of silver
arma, armōrum, n.pl.	arms, weapons
arrogantia, arrogantiae, f.	cheek, arrogance
*ars, artis, f.	art, skill
artifex, artificis, m.	artist, craftsman
as, assis, m.	as (small coin)
*ascendō, ascendere, ascendī	climb, rise
*at	but
Athēnae, Athēnārum, f.pl.	Athens
Athēnīs	at Athens
*atque	and
ātrium, ātriī, n.	atrium, main room, hall
*attonitus, attonita, attonitum	astonished
*auctor, auctōris, m.	creator, originator, person responsible
* mē auctōre	at my suggestion
*auctōritās, auctōritātis, f.	authority
*audācia, audāciae, f.	boldness, audacity
audācter	boldly
*audāx, *gen.* audācis	bold, daring
*audeō, audēre	dare
*audiō, audīre, audīvī, audītus	hear, listen to
*auferō, auferre, abstulī, ablātus	take away, steal
augeō, augēre, auxī, auctus	increase
*aula, aulae, f.	palace
aureus, aurea, aureum	gilded, gold-plated, golden, made of gold
aurīga, aurīgae, m.	charioteer
auris, auris, f.	ear

*autem	but
*auxilium, auxiliī, n.	help
avārus, avārī, m.	miser
avia, aviae, f.	grandmother
avidē	eagerly
avis, avis, f.	bird

——— b ———

balneum, balneī, n.	bath
barba, barbae, f.	beard
barbarus, barbarī, m.	barbarian
*bellum, bellī, n.	war
* bellum gerere	wage war, campaign
*bene	well
* optimē	very well
beneficium, beneficiī, n.	act of kindness, favour
*benignus, benigna, benignum	kind
*bibō, bibere, bibī	drink
blandus, blanda, blandum	flattering
*bonus, bona, bonum	good
* melior, melius	better
melius est	it would be better
* optimus, optima, optimum	very good, excellent, best
brevī	in a short time
*brevis, breve	short, brief
Britannī, Britannōrum, m.pl.	Britons
Britannia, Britanniae, f.	Britain

——— c ———

C. = Gāius	
*caelum, caelī, n.	sky, heaven
calceus, calceī, m.	shoe
calliditās, calliditātis, f.	cleverness, shrewdness
*callidus, callida, callidum	clever, cunning, shrewd
candēlābrum, candēlābrī, n.	lampstand, candelabrum
candidātus, candidātī, m.	candidate
*canis, canis, m.	dog
*cantō, cantāre, cantāvī	sing, chant
tībiīs cantāre	play on the pipes
*capiō, capere, cēpī, captus	take, catch, capture
cōnsilium capere	make a plan, have an idea
Capitōlium, Capitōliī, n.	the Capitol
captīva, captīvae, f.	(female) prisoner, captive
*captīvus, captīvī, m.	prisoner, captive
*caput, capitis, n.	head
*carcer, carceris, m.	prison
carmen, carminis, n.	song
carnifex, carnificis, m.	executioner
*cārus, cāra, cārum	dear
castellum, castellī, n.	fort
*castra, castrōrum, n.pl.	camp

cāsus, cāsūs, m.	*misfortune*
catēna, catēnae, f.	*chain*
caudex, caudicis, m.	*blockhead, idiot*
cautē	*cautiously*
caveō, cavēre, cāvī	*beware*
*cēdō, cēdere, cessī	*give in, give way, make way*
celebrō, celebrāre, celebrāvī, celebrātus	*celebrate*
*celeriter	*quickly, fast*
quam celerrimē	*as quickly as possible*
cellārius, cellāriī, m.	*steward*
*cēlō, cēlāre, cēlāvī, cēlātus	*hide*
*cēna, cēnae, f.	*dinner*
*cēnō, cēnāre, cēnāvī	*dine, have dinner*
*centum	*a hundred*
centuriō, centuriōnis, m.	*centurion*
cēpī *see* capiō	
certē	*certainly*
certō, certāre, certāvī	*compete*
*cēterī, cēterae, cētera, pl.	*the others, the rest*
Chrīstiānī, Chrīstiānōrum, m.pl.	*Christians*
*cibus, cibī, m.	*food*
circā + *acc.*	*around*
circiter + *acc.*	*about*
circulus, circulī, m.	*hoop*
*circum + *acc.*	*around*
*circumspectō, circumspectāre, circumspectāvī	*look round*
*circumveniō, circumvenīre, circumvēnī, circumventus	*surround*
circus, circī, m.	*circus, stadium*
Circus Maximus	*the Circus Maximus (stadium for chariot racing)*
citharoedus, citharoedī, m.	*cithara player*
*cīvis, cīvis, m.f.	*citizen*
clādēs, clādis, f.	*disaster*
*clāmō, clāmāre, clāmāvī	*shout*
*clāmor, clāmōris, m.	*shout, uproar*
*clārus, clāra, clārum	*famous, distinguished*
*claudō, claudere, clausī, clausus	*shut, close, block, conclude, complete*
cliēns, clientis, m.	*client*
*coepī	*I began*
*cōgitō, cōgitāre, cōgitāvī	*think, consider*
*cognōscō, cognōscere, cognōvī, cognitus	*get to know, find out*
*cōgō, cōgere, coēgī, coāctus	*force, compel*
colligō, colligere, collēgī, collēctus	*gather, collect, assemble*
collocō, collocāre, collocāvī, collocātus	*place, put*
columba, columbae, f.	*dove*
columna, columnae, f.	*pillar, column*
*comes, comitis, m.f.	*comrade, companion*
cōmiter	*politely, courteously*
*comitor, comitārī, comitātus sum	*accompany*
comitāns, *gen.* comitantis	*accompanying*

commemorō, commemorāre, commemorāvī, commemorātus	*talk about, mention, recall*
commendō, commendāre, commendāvī, commendātus	*recommend*
committō, committere, commīsī, commissus	*commit, begin*
*commodus, commoda, commodum	*convenient*
*commōtus, commōta, commōtum	*moved, alarmed, excited, distressed, upset*
*comparō, comparāre, comparāvī, comparātus	*obtain*
*compleō, complēre, complēvī, complētus	*fill*
compluvium, compluviī, n.	*compluvium (opening in roof)*
*compōnō, compōnere, composuī, compositus	*put together, arrange, settle, mix, make up*
compositus, composita, compositum	*composed, steady*
*comprehendō, comprehendere, comprehendī, comprehēnsus	*arrest, seize*
cōnātus *see* cōnor	
conclāve, conclāvis, n.	*room*
concrepō, concrepāre, concrepuī	*snap, click*
condūcō, condūcere, condūxī, conductus	*hire*
*cōnficiō, cōnficere, cōnfēcī, cōnfectus	*finish*
cōnfectus, cōnfecta, cōnfectum	*worn out, exhausted, overcome*
*cōnfīdō, cōnfīdere	*trust, put trust*
cōnfīsus, cōnfīsa, cōnfīsum	*having trusted, having put trust*
*coniciō, conicere, coniēcī, coniectus	*hurl, throw*
*cōnor, cōnārī, cōnātus sum	*try*
cōnscendō, cōnscendere, cōnscendī	*climb on, embark on, go on board, mount*
*cōnsentiō, cōnsentīre, cōnsēnsī	*agree*
cōnsīdō, cōnsīdere, cōnsēdī	*sit down*
*cōnsilium, cōnsiliī, n.	*plan, idea, advice*
cōnsilium capere	*make a plan, have an idea*
*cōnsistō, cōnsistere, cōnstitī	*stand one's ground, stand firm, halt, stop*
*cōnspiciō, cōnspicere, cōnspexī, cōnspectus	*catch sight of*
*cōnspicor, cōnspicārī, cōnspicātus sum	*catch sight of*

cōnspicuus, cōnspicua, cōnspicuum	conspicuous, easily seen		

cōnspicuus, cōnspicua,
cōnspicuum — *conspicuous, easily seen*
*cōnstituō, cōnstituere,
cōnstituī, cōnstitūtus — *decide*
cōnsul, cōnsulis, m. — *consul (senior magistrate)*
cōnsulātus, cōnsulātūs, m. — *consulship (rank of consul)*
*cōnsulō, cōnsulere, cōnsuluī,
cōnsultus — *consult*
*cōnsūmō, cōnsūmere,
cōnsūmpsī, cōnsūmptus — *eat*
*contendō, contendere,
contendī — *hurry*
*contentus, contenta,
contentum — *satisfied*
continuus, continua,
continuum — *continuous, on end*
*contrā + *acc.* — (1) *against*
*contrā — (2) *on the other hand*
contumēlia, contumēliae, f. — *insult, abuse*
*conveniō, convenīre, convēnī — *come together, gather, meet*
*convertō, convertere,
convertī, conversus — *turn*
convertor, convertī,
conversus sum — *turn*
convolvō, convolvere,
convolvī, convolūtus — *entangle*
*coquō, coquere, coxī, coctus — *cook*
*coquus, coquī, m. — *cook*
corōna, corōnae, f. — *garland, wreath*
*corpus, corporis, n. — *body*
corrumpō, corrumpere,
corrūpī, corruptus — *corrupt*
   dōnīs corrumpere — *bribe*
*cotīdiē — *every day*
*crās — *tomorrow*
*crēdō, crēdere, crēdidī — *trust, believe, have faith in*
creō, creāre, creāvī, creātus — *make, create*
*crūdēlis, crūdēle — *cruel*
crux, crucis, f. — *cross*
*cubiculum, cubiculī, n. — *bedroom*
cucurrī *see* currō
cui, cuius *see* quī
culīna, culīnae, f. — *kitchen*
culpō, culpāre, culpāvī — *blame*
culter, cultrī, m. — *knife*
*cum — (1) *when*
*cum + *abl.* — (2) *with*
cumulō, cumulāre, cumulāvī,
cumulātus — *heap*
*cupiō, cupere, cupīvī — *want*
*cūr? — *why?*
*cūra, cūrae, f. — *care*
   cūrae esse — *be a matter of concern*
cūria, cūriae, f. — *senate-house*
*cūrō, cūrāre, cūrāvī — *look after, supervise*
*currō, currere, cucurrī — *run*
currus, currūs, m. — *chariot*
*custōdiō, custōdīre,
custōdīvī, custōdītus — *guard*
*custōs, custōdis, m. — *guard*

——— **d** ———

damnō, damnāre, damnāvī,
damnātus — *condemn*
dare *see* dō
*dē + *abl.* — *from, down from; about*
*dea, deae, f. — *goddess*
*dēbeō, dēbēre, dēbuī,
dēbitus — *owe, ought, should, must*
*decem — *ten*
*dēcidō, dēcidere, dēcidī — *fall down*
decimus, decima, decimum — *tenth*
*dēcipiō, dēcipere, dēcēpī,
dēceptus — *deceive, fool*
dēclārō, dēclārāre, dēclārāvī,
dēclārātus — *declare, proclaim*
*decōrus, decōra, decōrum — *right, proper*
dedī *see* dō
dēdicō, dēdicāre, dēdicāvī,
dēdicātus — *dedicate*
dēdūcō, dēdūcere, dēdūxī,
dēductus — *escort*
*dēfendō, dēfendere, dēfendī,
dēfēnsus — *defend*
dēfīgō, dēfīgere, dēfīxī,
dēfixus — *fix*
dēiciō, dēicere, dēiēcī,
dēiectus — *throw down, throw*
dēiectus, dēiecta,
dēiectum — *disappointed*
*deinde — *then*
*dēlectō, dēlectāre, dēlectāvī,
dēlectātus — *delight, please*
*dēleō, dēlēre, dēlēvī, dēlētus — *destroy*
dēliciae, dēliciārum, f.pl. — *darling*
dēligō, dēligāre, dēligāvī,
dēligātus — *bind, tie, tie up, moor*
*dēmittō, dēmittere, dēmīsī,
dēmissus — *let down, lower*
*dēmōnstrō, dēmōnstrāre,
dēmōnstrāvī, dēmōnstrātus — *point out, show*
dēmoveō, dēmovēre, dēmōvī,
dēmōtus — *dismiss, move out of the way*
dēmum — *at last*
   tum dēmum — *then at last, only then*
dēnārius, dēnāriī, m. — *a denarius (coin worth four sesterces)*
*dēnique — *at last, finally*
dēns, dentis, m. — *tooth*
dēnsus, dēnsa, dēnsum — *thick*
dēpellō, dēpellere, dēpulī,
dēpulsus — *drive off, push down*
dēpōnō, dēpōnere, dēposuī,
dēpositus — *put down, take off*
dērīdeō, dērīdēre, dērīsī,
dērīsus — *mock, jeer at*
*dēscendō, dēscendere,
dēscendī — *come down, go down*

* dēserō, dēserere, dēseruī,
    dēsertus   *desert*
  dēsiliō, dēsilīre, dēsiluī   *jump down*
  dēsinō, dēsinere   *end, cease*
  dēsistō, dēsistere, dēstitī   *stop*
* dēspērō, dēspērāre,
    dēspērāvī   *despair, give up*
  dēspiciō, dēspicere, dēspexī   *look down*
  dētestor, dētestārī,
    dētestātus sum   *curse*
  dētrahō, dētrahere, dētrāxī,
    dētractus   *pull down*
* deus, deī, m.   *god*
      dī immortālēs!   *heavens above!*
  dēvorō, dēvorāre, dēvorāvī,
    dēvorātus   *devour, eat up*
  diabolus, diabolī, m.   *devil*
* dīcō, dīcere, dīxī, dictus   *say*
* diēs, diēī, m.   *day*
    diēs fēstus, diēī fēstī, m.   *festival, holiday*
    diēs nātālis,
      diēī nātālis, m.   *birthday*
* difficilis, difficile   *difficult*
  difficultās, difficultātis, f.   *difficulty*
  digitus, digitī, m.   *finger*
* dignitās, dignitātis, f.   *dignity, importance, prestige*
* dīligenter   *carefully, diligently*
    dīligentius   *more diligently, harder*
  dīligō, dīligere, dīlēxī,
    dīlēctus   *be fond of*
  dīmittō, dīmittere, dīmīsī,
    dīmissus   *send away, dismiss*
  dīripiō, dīripere, dīripuī,
    dīreptus   *pull apart, ransack*
* dīrus, dīra, dīrum   *dreadful*
  dīs *see* deus
* discēdō, discēdere, discessī   *depart, leave*
  discipulus, discipulī, m.   *disciple, follower*
  discō, discere, didicī   *learn*
  discordia, discordiae, f.   *strife*
  discrīmen, discrīminis, n.   *crisis*
  dissimulō, dissimulāre,
    dissimulāvī, dissimulātus   *conceal, hide*
  distribuō, distribuere,
    distribuī, distribūtus   *distribute*
* diū   *for a long time*
    diūtius   *any longer*
* dīves, *gen.* dīvitis   *rich*
    dītissimus, dītissima,
      dītissimum   *very rich*
* dīvitiae, dīvitiārum, f.pl   *riches*
  dīvus, dīvī, m.   *god*
  dīxī *see* dīcō
* dō, dare, dedī, datus   *give*
*   poenās dare   *pay the penalty, be punished*
* doceō, docēre, docuī, doctus   *teach*
*   doctus, docta, doctum   *learned, educated, skilful,*
                        clever
* doleō, dolēre, doluī   *hurt, be in pain*
* dolor, dolōris, m.   *pain, grief*

* domina, dominae, f.   *mistress, madam*
* dominus, dominī, m.   *master*
* domus, domūs, f.   *house, home*
    domī   *at home*
    domum redīre   *return home*
* dōnum, dōnī, n.   *present, gift*
    dōnīs corrumpere   *bribe*
* dormiō, dormīre, dormīvī   *sleep*
  dubium, dubiī, n.   *doubt*
* dūcō, dūcere, dūxī, ductus   *lead, take*
    sorte ductus   *chosen by lot*
* dum   *while, until*
* duo, duae, duo   *two*
  duodecim   *twelve*
* dūrus, dūra, dūrum   *harsh, hard*
* dux, ducis, m.   *leader*
  dūxī *see* dūcō

e

* ē, ex + *abl.*   *from, out of*
  ea, eā, eam *see* is
  eādem, eandem   *the same*
  eās *see* is
  ēbrius, ēbria, ēbrium   *drunk*
* ecce!   *see! look!*
  edō, edere, ēdī, ēsus   *eat*
  ēdūcō, ēdūcere, ēdūxī,
    ēductus   *lead out*
  efferō, efferre, extulī, ēlātus   *bring out, carry out*
* efficiō, efficere, effēcī,
    effectus   *carry out, accomplish*
  effigiēs, effigiēī, f.   *image, statue*
  effringō, effringere, effrēgī,
    effrāctus   *break down*
* effugiō, effugere, effūgī   *escape*
* effundō, effundere, effūdī,
    effūsus   *pour out*
    effūsīs lacrimīs   *with tears pouring out,*
                        bursting into tears
  ēgī *see* agō
* ego, meī   *I, me*
* ēgredior, ēgredī,
    ēgressus sum   *go out*
* ēheu!   *oh dear! oh no!*
  eī *see* is
* ēiciō, ēicere, ēiēcī, ēiectus   *throw out*
  eīs, eius *see* is
  eiusmodī   *of that kind*
  ēlābor, ēlābī, ēlāpsus sum   *slip out, escape*
  ēlegāns, *gen.* ēlegantis   *tasteful, elegant*
  ēlegantia, ēlegantiae, f.   *good taste, elegance*
  ēliciō, ēlicere, ēlicuī, ēlicitus   *lure, entice*
* ēligō, ēligere, ēlēgī, ēlēctus   *choose*
  ēlūdō, ēlūdere, ēlūdī, ēlūsus   *slip past, trick, outwit*
* ēmittō, ēmittere, ēmīsī,
    ēmissus   *throw, send out*

*emō, emere, ēmī, ēmptus	buy
ēmoveō, ēmovēre, ēmōvī, ēmōtus	move, clear away
ēn!	look!
ēn Rōmānī!	so these are the Romans!
*enim	for
*eō, īre, iī	go
obviam īre	meet, go to meet
eō see is	
eōdem	the same
eōrum, eōs see is	
*epistula, epistulae, f.	letter
epulae, epulārum, f.pl.	dishes
*eques, equitis, m.	horseman, well-to-do man ranking below senator
*equus, equī, m.	horse
eram see sum	
ergō	therefore
ērubēscō, ērubēscere, ērubuī	blush
ērumpō, ērumpere, ērūpī	break away, break out
est, estō see sum	
*et	and
* et ... et	both ... and
*etiam	even, also
nōn modo ... sed etiam	not only ... but also
eum see is	
evangelium, evangeliī, n.	good news, gospel
ēvertō, ēvertere, ēvertī, ēversus	overturn
ēvolō, ēvolāre, ēvolāvī	fly out
*ex, ē + abl.	from, out of
exanimātus, examināta, exanimātum	unconscious
*excipiō, excipere, excēpī, exceptus	receive
*excitō, excitāre, excitāvī, excitātus	arouse, wake up
*exclāmō, exclāmāre, exclāmāvī	exclaim, shout
exemplum, exemplī, n.	example
*exeō, exīre, exiī	go out
exīstimō, exīstimāre, exīstimāvī, exīstimātus	think, consider
exitium, exitiī, n.	ruin, destruction
*explicō, explicāre, explicāvī, explicātus	explain
expōnō, expōnere, exposuī, expositus	unload
expugnō, expugnāre, expugnāvī, expugnātus	storm, take by storm
exquīsītus, exquīsīta, exquīsītum	special
*exspectō, exspectāre, exspectāvī, exspectātus	wait for
exstinguō, exstinguere, exstīnxī, exstīnctus	extinguish, destroy
exstruō, exstruere, exstrūxī, exstrūctus	build
exsultō, exsultāre, exsultāvī	exult, be triumphant
exta, extōrum, n.pl.	entrails

*extrā	outside
extrahō, extrahere, extrāxī, extractus	drag out, pull out, take out
extrēmus, extrēma, extrēmum	furthest
extrēma pars	edge
extulī see efferō	

—————— **f** ——————

*faber, fabrī, m.	craftsman, workman
*fābula, fābulae, f.	story, play
fābulam agere	act a play
facēs see fax	
*facile	easily
*facilis, facile	easy
facinus, facinoris, n.	crime
*faciō, facere, fēcī, factus	make, do
factum, factī, n.	deed, achievement
Falernus, Falerna, Falernum	Falernian
*falsus, falsa, falsum	false, untrue, dishonest
famēs, famis, f.	hunger
familiāris, familiāris, m.	close friend, relation, relative
faucēs, faucium, f.pl.	passage, entrance-way
*faveō, favēre, fāvī	favour, support
favor, favōris, m.	favour
fax, facis, f.	torch
fēcī see faciō	
fēlēs, fēlis, f.	cat
fēlīx, gen. fēlīcis	lucky
*fēmina, fēminae, f.	woman
*ferō, ferre, tulī, lātus	bring, carry
*ferōciter	fiercely
*ferōx, gen. ferōcis	fierce, ferocious
*fessus, fessa, fessum	tired
*festīnō, festīnāre, festīnāvī	hurry
fēstus, fēsta, fēstum	festival, holiday
*fidēlis, fidēle	faithful, loyal
*fidēs, fideī, f.	loyalty, trustworthiness
fidem servāre	keep a promise, keep faith
fīgō, fīgere, fīxī, fīxus	fix, fasten
figūra, figūrae, f.	figure, shape
*fīlia, fīliae, f.	daughter
*fīlius, fīliī, m.	son
fīxus see fīgō	
flagrō, flagrāre, flagrāvī	blaze
*flamma, flammae, f.	flame
*flōs, flōris, m.	flower
*flūmen, flūminis, n.	river
*fluō, fluere, flūxī	flow
*fōns, fontis, m.	fountain, spring
fōrma, fōrmae, f.	beauty, appearance
*fortasse	perhaps
*forte	by chance
*fortis, forte	brave
*fortiter	bravely
fortitūdō, fortitūdinis, f.	courage

fortūna, fortūnae, f.	fortune, luck
fortūnātus, fortūnāta, fortūnātum	lucky
forum, forī, n.	forum, market-place
fossa, fossae, f.	ditch
fragor, fragōris, m.	crash
*frangō, frangere, frēgī, frāctus	break
*frāter, frātris, m.	brother
frōns, frontis, f.	front
*frūmentum, frūmentī, n.	grain
*frūstrā	in vain
*fuga, fugae, f.	escape
*fugiō, fugere, fūgī	run away, flee (from)
fuī see sum	
fulgeō, fulgēre, fulsī	shine
*fundō, fundere, fūdī, fūsus	pour
*fundus, fundī, m.	farm
fūnis, fūnis, m.	rope
*fūr, fūris, m.	thief
furēns, gen. furentis	furious, in a rage
fūstis, fūstis, m.	club, stick

g

garriō, garrīre, garrīvī	chatter, gossip
*gaudeō, gaudēre	be pleased, rejoice
*gaudium, gaudiī, n.	joy
gāza, gāzae, f.	treasure
*gemitus, gemitūs, m.	groan
gemma, gemmae, f.	gem, jewel
*gēns, gentis, f.	family, tribe
*gerō, gerere, gessī, gestus	wear
* bellum gerere	wage war, campaign
gladiātor, gladiātōris, m.	gladiator
*gladius, gladiī, m.	sword
glōria, glōriae, f.	glory
glōriāns, gen. glōriantis	boasting, boastfully
Graecia, Graeciae, f.	Greece
Graecus, Graeca, Graecum	Greek
grātiae, grātiārum, f.pl.	thanks
* grātiās agere	give thanks, thank
grātīs	free
grātulātiō, grātulātiōnis, f.	congratulation
grātulor, grātulārī, grātulātus sum	congratulate
grātulāns, gen. grātulantis	congratulating
*gravis, grave	heavy, serious
*graviter	heavily, seriously, soundly

h

*habeō, habēre, habuī, habitus	have
*habitō, habitāre, habitāvī	live

haereō, haerēre, haesī	stick, cling
haesitō, haesitāre, haesitāvī	hesitate
haruspex, haruspicis, m.	soothsayer
*hasta, hastae, f.	spear
Hateriānus, Hateriāna, Hateriānum	belonging to Haterius
*haud	not
*haudquāquam	not at all
hercle!	by Hercules! good heavens!
*heri	yesterday
*hic, haec, hoc	this
*hīc	here
hinc	from here
*hodiē	today
*homō, hominis, m.	human being, man
homunculus, homunculī, m.	little man
*honor, honōris, m.	honour, public position
honōrō, honōrāre, honōrāvī, honōrātus	honour
*hōra, hōrae, f.	hour
horreum, horreī, n.	barn, granary
*hortor, hortārī, hortātus sum	encourage, urge
*hortus, hortī, m.	garden
*hospes, hospitis, m.	guest, host
*hostis, hostis, m.f.	enemy
*hūc	here, to this place
hūc illūc	here and there, up and down
huic, huius see hic	
humilis, humile	low-born, of low class
humus, humī, f.	ground
* humī	on the ground
humum	to the ground

i

*iaceō, iacēre, iacuī	lie
*iaciō, iacere, iēcī, iactus	throw
*iactō, iactāre, iactāvī, iactātus	throw
*iam	now
iamdūdum	for a long time
*iānua, iānuae, f.	door
ībam see eō	
*ibi	there
id see is	
*īdem, eadem, idem	the same
*identidem	repeatedly
Ierosolyma, Ierosolymae, f.	Jerusalem
*igitur	therefore, and so
*ignārus, ignāra, ignārum	not knowing, unaware
*ignāvus, ignāva, ignāvum	lazy, cowardly
ignis, ignis, m.	fire
ignōrō, ignōrāre, ignōrāvī	not know about
*ignōscō, ignōscere, ignōvī	forgive
iī see eō	
*ille, illa, illud	that, he, she
illūc	there, to that place
hūc illūc	here and there, up and down

illūcēscō, illūcēscere, illūxī   *dawn, grow bright*
imitor, imitārī, imitātus sum   *imitate, mime*
immineō, imminēre, imminuī   *hang over*
immo   *or rather*
immortālis, immortāle   *immortal*
    dī immortālēs!   *heavens above!*
immortālitās,
    immortālitātis, f.   *immortality*
*immōtus, immōta, immōtum   *still, motionless*
impatiēns, *gen.* impatientis   *impatient*
    morae impatiēns   *impatient at the delay*
*impediō, impedīre,
    impedīvī, impedītus   *delay, hinder*
*imperātor, imperātōris, m.   *emperor*
*imperium, imperiī, n.   *empire*
*imperō, imperāre, imperāvī   *order, command*
importō, importāre,
    importāvī, importātus   *import*
impudēns, *gen.* impudentis   *shameless*
*in + *acc.*   **(1)** *into, onto*
*in + *abl.*   **(2)** *in, on*
*incēdō, incēdere, incessī   *march, stride*
*incendō, incendere, incendī,
    incēnsus   *burn, set on fire, set fire to*
incertus, incerta, incertum   *uncertain*
incidō, incidere, incidī   *fall*
*incipiō, incipere, incēpī,
    inceptus   *begin*
incitō, incitāre, incitāvī,
    incitātus   *urge on, encourage*
inde   *then*
indicium, indiciī, n.   *sign, evidence*
indignus, indigna, indignum   *unworthy, undeserved*
*infēlīx, *gen.* infēlīcis   *unlucky*
*inferō, inferre, intulī, inlātus   *bring in, bring on*
    iniūriam inferre   *do an injustice to, bring injury to*
īnfīgō, īnfīgere, īnfīxī,
    īnfīxus   *fasten onto*
īnflīgō, īnflīgere, īnflīxī,
    īnflīctus   *inflict*
īnflō, īnflāre, īnflāvī   *blow*
īnfundō, īnfundere, īnfūdī,
    īnfūsus   *pour into*
*ingēns, *gen.* ingentis   *huge*
*ingredior, ingredī,
    ingressus sum   *enter*
iniciō, inicere, iniēcī, iniectus   *throw in*
inimīcus, inimīcī, m.   *enemy*
*iniūria, iniūriae, f.   *injustice, injury*
    iniūriam inferre   *do an injustice to, bring injury to*
inlātus *see* inferō
inopia, inopiae, f.   *poverty*
*inquit   *says, said*
īnsāniō, īnsānīre, īnsānīvī   *be mad, be insane*
īnsānus, īnsāna, īnsānum   *mad, crazy*
īnscrībō, īnscrībere,
    īnscrīpsī, īnscrīptus   *write, inscribe*
*īnsidiae, īnsidiārum, f.pl.   *trap, ambush*

īnsolēns, *gen.* īnsolentis   *rude, insolent*
*īnspiciō, īnspicere, īnspexī,
    īnspectus   *look at, inspect, examine, search*
*īnstruō, īnstruere, īnstrūxī,
    īnstrūctus   *draw up, set up*
*īnsula, īnsulae, f.   *island; block of flats, apartment building*
*intellegō, intellegere,
    intellēxī, intellēctus   *understand*
*intentē   *closely, carefully*
*inter + *acc.*   *among, between*
    inter sē   *among themselves, with each other*
*intereā   *meanwhile*
*interficiō, interficere,
    interfēcī, interfectus   *kill*
interrogō, interrogāre,
    interrogāvī, interrogātus   *question*
interrumpō, interrumpere,
    interrūpī, interruptus   *interrupt*
*intrō, intrāre, intrāvī   *enter*
intulī *see* īnferō
*inveniō, invenīre, invēnī,
    inventus   *find*
invicem   *in turn*
*invītō, invītāre, invītāvī,
    invītātus   *invite*
*invītus, invīta, invītum   *unwilling, reluctant*
iocus, iocī, m.   *joke*
Iovis *see* Iuppiter
*ipse, ipsa, ipsum   *himself, herself, itself*
*īra, īrae, f.   *anger*
*īrātus, īrāta, īrātum   *angry*
īre *see* eō
irrumpō, irrumpere, irrūpī,
    irruptus   *burst in, burst into*
*is, ea, id   *he, she, it*
*iste, ista, istud   *that*
*ita   *in this way*
*   ita vērō   *yes*
Ītalia, Ītaliae, f.   *Italy*
*itaque   *and so*
*iter, itineris, n.   *journey, progress*
*iterum   *again*
*iubeō, iubēre, iussī, iussus   *order*
Iūdaeī, Iūdaeōrum, m.pl.   *Jews*
Iūdaeus, Iūdaea, Iūdaeum   *Jewish*
*iūdex, iūdicis, m.   *judge*
iūdicō, iūdicāre, iūdicāvī,
    iūdicātus   *judge*
iugulum, iugulī, n.   *throat*
Iuppiter, Iovis, m.   *Jupiter (god of the sky, greatest of Roman gods)*
iussī *see* iubeō
*iussum, iussī, n.   *instruction, order*
    iussū Silvae   *at Silva's order*
iuvat, iuvāre   *please*
    mē iuvat   *it pleases me*
*iuvenis, iuvenis, m.   *young man*
iuxtā + *acc.*   *next to*

l

L. = Lūcius

lābor, lābī, lāpsus sum	*fall*
*labor, labōris, m.	*work, labour*
*labōrō, labōrāre, labōrāvī	*work*
labrum, labrī, n.	*lip*
*lacrima, lacrimae, f.	*tear*
lacrimīs effūsīs	*with tears pouring out, bursting into tears*
*lacrimō, lacrimāre, lacrimāvī	*weep, cry*
lacus, lacūs, m.	*lake*
laetē	*happily*
*laetus, laeta, laetum	*happy*
lānx, lancis, f.	*dish*
lāpsus *see* lābor	
latebrae, latebrārum, f.pl.	*hiding-place*
*lateō, latēre, latuī	*lie hidden*
later, lateris, m.	*brick*
latrō, latrōnis, m.	*robber, thug*
*laudō, laudāre, laudāvī, laudātus	*praise*
lectīca, lectīcae, f.	*litter*
*lectus, lectī, m.	*couch, bed*
*lēgātus, lēgātī, m.	*commander*
*legiō, legiōnis, f.	*legion*
*legō, legere, lēgī, lēctus	*read*
lēniō, lēnīre, lēnīvī, lēnītus	*soothe, calm down*
lēniter	*gently*
*lentē	*slowly*
*leō, leōnis, m.	*lion*
*libenter	*gladly*
*liber, librī, m.	*book*
*līberālis, līberāle	*generous*
*līberī, līberōrum, m.pl.	*children*
*līberō, līberāre, līberāvī, līberātus	*free, set free*
*lībertās, lībertātis, f.	*freedom*
*lībertus, lībertī, m.	*freedman, ex-slave*
Augustī lībertus	*freedman of Augustus, freedman of the emperor*
līmen, līminis, n.	*threshold, doorway*
littera, litterae, f.	*letter*
*lītus, lītoris, n.	*sea-shore, shore*
*locus, locī, m.	*place*
longurius, longuriī, m.	*pole*
longus, longa, longum	*long*
*loquor, loquī, locūtus sum	*speak*
lūbricus, lūbrica, lūbricum	*slippery*
lūcem *see* lūx	
lūceō, lūcēre, lūxī	*shine*
lucerna, lucernae, f.	*lamp*
lūdō, lūdere, lūsī	*play*
*lūdus, lūdī, m.	*game*
lūgeō, lūgēre, lūxī	*lament, mourn, grieve*
*lūna, lūnae, f.	*moon*
lutum, lutī, n.	*mud*
*lūx, lūcis, f.	*light, daylight*

m

M. = Marcus

magister, magistrī, m.	*foreman*
magistrātus, magistrātūs, m.	*magistrate (elected official)*
magnificē	*splendidly, magnificently*
magnificus, magnifica, magnificum	*splendid, magnificent*
*magnopere	*greatly*
* maximē	*very greatly, very much, most of all*
*magnus, magna, magnum	*big, large, great*
maior, *gen.* maiōris	*bigger, larger, greater*
* maximus, maxima, maximum	*very big, very large, very great, greatest*
Circus Maximus	*the Circus Maximus (stadium for chariot racing)*
malignus, maligna, malignum	*spiteful*
*mālō, mālle, māluī	*prefer*
*malus, mala, malum	*evil, bad*
peior, *gen.* peiōris	*worse*
* pessimus, pessima, pessimum	*worst, very bad*
*mandātum, mandātī, n.	*instruction, order*
*mandō, mandāre, mandāvī, mandātus	*order, entrust, hand over*
*māne	*in the morning*
*maneō, manēre, mānsī	*remain, stay*
*manus, manūs, f.	**(1)** *hand*
*manus, manūs, f.	**(2)** *band (of men)*
*mare, maris, n.	*sea*
margō, marginis, m.	*edge*
*marītus, marītī, m.	*husband*
marmor, marmoris, n.	*marble*
Mārs, Mārtis, m.	*Mars (god of war)*
massa, massae, f.	*block*
*māter, mātris, f.	*mother*
mātrōna, mātrōnae, f.	*lady*
maximē *see* magnopere	
maximus *see* magnus	
mē *see* ego	
medicāmentum, medicāmentī, n.	*ointment, medicine, drug*
medicus, medicī, m.	*doctor*
*medius, media, medium	*middle*
melior *see* bonus	
memor, *gen.* memoris	*remembering, mindful of*
*mendāx, mendācis, m.	*liar*
mendīcus, mendīcī, m.	*beggar*
mēns, mentis, f.	*mind*
*mēnsa, mēnsae, f.	*table*
*mercātor, mercātōris, m.	*merchant*
*metus, metūs, m.	*fear*
*meus, mea, meum	*my, mine*
meī, meōrum, m.pl.	*my family*
mī Haterī	*my dear Haterius*

mihi *see* ego
*mīles, mīlitis, m. — soldier
*mīlle — a thousand
* mīlia — thousands
*minimē — no, least, very little
minor *see* parvus
minor, minārī, minātus sum — threaten
*mīrābilis, mīrābile — extraordinary, strange, marvellous
mīrus, mīra, mīrum — extraordinary
*miser, misera, miserum — miserable, wretched, sad
*mittō, mittere, mīsī, missus — send
*modo — just, now, only
modo ... modo — now ... now
nōn modo ... sed etiam — not only ... but also
*modus, modī, m. — manner, way, kind
eiusmodī — of that kind
eōdem modō — in the same way
* quō modō? — how? in what way?
molliō, mollīre, mollīvī, mollītus — soothe
mollis, molle — soft, gentle
*moneō, monēre, monuī, monitus — warn, advise
*mōns, montis, m. — mountain
mora, morae, f. — delay
*morbus, morbī, m. — illness
*morior, morī, mortuus sum — die
moriēns, *gen.* morientis — dying
* mortuus, mortua, mortuum — dead
moror, morārī, morātus sum — delay
*mors, mortis, f. — death
mortuus *see* morior
mōs, mōris, m. — custom
mōtus, mōtūs, m. — movement
*moveō, movēre, mōvī, mōtus — move
*mox — soon
multitūdō, multitūdinis, f. — crowd
multō — much
multum — much
*multus, multa, multum — much
* multī — many
* plūrimī, plūrimae, plūrima — very many
* plūrimus, plūrima, plūrimum — most
plūris est — is worth more
* plūs, *gen.* plūris — more
plūs vīnī — more wine
mūnītiō, mūnītiōnis, f. — defence, fortification
*mūrus, mūrī, m. — wall
mūs, mūris, m.f. — mouse
mussitō, mussitāre, mussitāvī — murmur

nactus, nacta, nactum — having seized
*nam — for
*nārrō, nārrāre, nārrāvī, nārrātus — tell, relate
*nāscor, nāscī, nātus sum — be born
nātū maximus — eldest
trīgintā annōs nātus — thirty years old
(diēs) nātālis, (diēī) nātālis, m. — birthday
* nātus, nāta, nātum — born
*nauta, nautae, m. — sailor
*nāvigō, nāvigāre, nāvigāvī — sail
*nāvis, nāvis, f. — ship
*nē — that ... not, so that ... not
* nē ... quidem — not even
*nec — and not, nor
* nec ... nec — neither ... nor
*necesse — necessary
*necō, necāre, necāvī, necātus — kill
neglegēns, *gen.* neglegentis — careless, taking no notice of
*neglegō, neglegere, neglēxī, neglēctus — neglect, ignore, disregard
*negōtium, negōtiī, n. — business
negōtium agere — do business, work
*nēmō — no one, nobody
neque — and not, nor
* neque ... neque — neither ... nor
*nescio, nescīre, nescīvī — not know
*nihil — nothing
nihilōminus — nevertheless
*nimis — too
*nimium — too much
*nisi — except, unless
*nōbilis, nōbile — noble, of noble birth
nōbīs *see* nōs
*noceō, nocēre, nocuī — hurt, harm
noctis *see* nox
*nōlō, nōlle, nōluī — not want
nōlī, nōlīte — do not, don't
*nōmen, nōminis, n. — name
*nōn — not
*nōnāgintā — ninety
nōndum — not yet
*nōnne? — surely?
*nōnnūllī, nōnnūllae, nōnnūlla — some, several
nōnus, nōna, nōnum — ninth
*nōs — we, us
*noster, nostra, nostrum — our
*nōtus, nōta, nōtum — known, well-known, famous
*novem — nine
*nōvī — I know
*novus, nova, novum — new
*nox, noctis, f. — night
nūllus, nūlla, nūllum — not any, no
*num? — (1) surely ... not?
*num — (2) whether

*numerus, numerī, m.	number	orior, orīrī, ortus sum	rise
*numquam	never	ōrnāmentum, ōrnāmentī, n.	ornament, decoration
*nunc	now	ōrnāmenta praetōria	honorary praetorship,
*nūntiō, nūntiāre, nūntiāvī,			honorary rank of praetor
nūntiātus	announce	ōrnātus, ōrnāta, ōrnātum	decorated, elaborately furnished
*nūntius, nūntiī, m.	messenger, news	*ōrnō, ōrnāre, ōrnāvī, ōrnātus	decorate
*nūper	recently	*ōrō, ōrāre, ōrāvī	beg
nusquam	nowhere	ortus see orior	
		ōs, ōris, n.	face
		ōsculum, ōsculī, n.	kiss
		*ostendō, ostendere, ostendī,	
		ostentus	show
		ostentō, ostentāre, ostentāvī,	
		ostentātus	show off, display
		*ōtiōsus, ōtiōsa, ōtiōsum	idle, on holiday

—————— **o** ——————

obeō, obīre, obiī	meet, go to meet
obēsus, obēsa, obēsum	fat
obiciō, obicere, obiēcī,	
obiectus	present
oblītus, oblīta, oblītum	having forgotten
obscūrus, obscūra, obscūrum	dark, gloomy
*obstō, obstāre, obstitī	obstruct, block the way
obstupefaciō, obstupefacere,	
obstupefēcī, obstupefactus	amaze, stun
obtulī see offerō	
obviam eō, obviam īre,	
obviam iī	meet, go to meet
occāsiō, occāsiōnis, f.	opportunity
*occīdō, occīdere, occīdī,	
occīsus	kill
occidō, occidere, occidī	set
occupātus, occupāta,	
occupātum	busy
occupō, occupāre, occupāvī,	
occupātus	seize, take over
octāvus, octāva, octāvum	eighth
*octō	eight
*octōgintā	eighty
*oculus, oculī, m.	eye
*ōdī	I hate
odiō sum, odiō esse	be hateful
*offerō, offerre, obtulī, oblātus	offer
oleum, oleī, n.	oil
*ōlim	once, some time ago
ōmen, ōminis, n.	omen (sign from the gods)
*omnīnō	completely
*omnis, omne	all
omnia	all, everything
*opēs, opum, f.pl.	money, wealth
*oppidum, oppidī, n.	town
*opprimō, opprimere,	
oppressī, oppressus	crush
*oppugnō, oppugnāre,	
oppugnāvī, oppugnātus	attack
optimē see bene	
optimus see bonus	
*opus, operis, n.	work, construction
ōrātiō, ōrātiōnis, f.	speech
orbis, orbis, m.	globe
orbis terrārum	world
ōrdō, ōrdinis, m.	row, line

—————— **p** ——————

*paene	nearly, almost
pallēscō, pallēscere, palluī	grow pale
pantomīmus, pantomīmī, m.	pantomimus, dancer
*parcō, parcere, pepercī	spare
*pāreō, pārēre, pāruī	obey
*parō, parāre, parāvī, parātus	prepare
*pars, partis, f.	part
extrēma pars	edge
prīmā in parte	in the forefront
*parvus, parva, parvum	small, little
minor, gen. minōris	less, smaller
* minimus, minima,	
minimum	very little, least
passus see patior	
*patefaciō, patefacere,	
patefēcī, patefactus	reveal
*pater, patris, m.	father
*patior, patī, passus sum	suffer, endure
patrōnus, patrōnī, m.	patron
*paucī, paucae, pauca	few, a few
paulīsper	for a short time
paulō	a little
*pauper, gen. pauperis	poor
pauper, pauperis, m.	a poor man
*pavor, pavōris, m.	panic
*pāx, pācis, f.	peace
*pecūnia, pecūniae, f.	money
pedem see pēs	
peior see malus	
pendeō, pendēre, pependī	hang
*per + acc.	through, along
percutiō, percutere, percussī,	
percussus	strike
*pereō, perīre, periī	die, perish
*perficiō, perficere, perfēcī,	
perfectus	finish
perfidus, perfida, perfidum	treacherous, untrustworthy
perfodiō, perfodere, perfōdī,	
perfossus	pick (teeth)

perīculōsus, perīculōsa,
   perīculōsum   *dangerous*
*perīculum, perīculī, n.   *danger*
perii *see* pereō
perītē   *skilfully*
*perītus, perīta, perītum   *skilful*
perpetuus, perpetua,
   perpetuum   *perpetual, everlasting*
   in perpetuum   *for ever*
perstō, perstāre, perstitī   *persist*
*persuādeō, persuādēre,
   persuāsī   *persuade*
*perterreō, perterrēre,
   perterruī, perterritus   *terrify*
perturbō, perturbāre,
   perturbāvī, perturbātus   *disturb, alarm*
*perveniō, pervenīre, pervēnī *reach, arrive at*
*pēs, pedis, m.   *foot, paw*
   pedem referre   *step back*
pessimus *see* malus
petauristārius,
   petauristāriī, m.   *acrobat*
*petō, petere, petīvī, petītus *make for, attack; seek, beg for, ask*
                     for
philosopha, philosophae, f. *(female) philosopher*
philosophia, philosophiae, f. *philosophy*
philosophus, philosophī, m. *philosopher*
pīpiō, pīpiāre, pīpiāvī   *chirp*
*placeō, placēre, placuī   *please, suit*
*plaudō, plaudere, plausī,
   plausus   *applaud, clap*
plaustrum, plaustrī, n.   *wagon, cart*
plausus, plausūs, m.   *applause*
*plēnus, plēna, plēnum   *full*
pluit, pluere, pluit   *rain*
plūrimus, plūs *see* multus
pōculum, pōculī, n.   *wine-cup*
*poena, poenae, f.   *punishment*
*   poenās dare   *pay the penalty, be punished*
*poēta, poētae, m.   *poet*
polliceor, pollicērī,
   pollicitus sum   *promise*
polyspaston, polyspastī, n. *crane*
pompa, pompae, f.   *procession*
*pōnō, pōnere, posuī, positus *place, put, put up*
*pōns, pontis, m.   *bridge*
poposcī *see* poscō
*populus, populī, m.   *people*
*porta, portae, f.   *gate*
porticus, porticūs, f.   *colonnade*
*portō, portāre, portāvī,
   portātus   *carry*
*portus, portūs, m.   *harbour*
*poscō, poscere, poposcī   *demand, ask for*
positus *see* pōnō
possideō, possidēre, possēdī,
   possessus   *possess*
*possum, posse, potuī   *can, be able*
*post + *acc.*   *after, behind*
*posteā   *afterwards*

posterī, posterōrum, m.pl. *future generations, posterity*
postīcum, postīcī, n.   *back gate*
*postquam   *after, when*
postrēmō   *finally, lastly*
*postrīdiē   *on the next day*
*postulō, postulāre, postulāvī,
   postulātus   *demand*
posuī *see* pōnō
*potestās, potestātis, f.   *power*
potius   *rather*
potuī *see* possum
*praebeō, praebēre, praebuī,
   praebitus   *offer, provide*
*praeceps, *gen.* praecipitis *headlong*
praecipitō, praecipitāre,
   praecipitāvī   *hurl*
   sē praecipitāre   *hurl oneself*
praecō, praecōnis, m.   *herald, announcer*
praedīcō, praedīcere,
   praedīxī, praedictus   *foretell, predict*
praeficiō, praeficere,
   praefēcī, praefectus   *put in charge*
*praemium, praemiī, n.   *prize, reward, profit*
praeruptus, praerupta,
   praeruptum   *sheer, steep*
praesēns, *gen.* praesentis *present, ready*
praesertim   *especially*
praestō, praestāre, praestitī *show, display*
praesum, praeesse, praefuī *be in charge of*
praeter + *acc.*   *except*
praetereō, praeterīre,
   praeteriī   *go past*
praetōriānus, praetōriānī, m. *praetorian (belonging to the*
                   emperor's bodyguard)
praetōrius, praetōria,
   praetōrium   *praetorian*
   ōrnāmenta praetōria   *honorary praetorship,*
                  honorary rank of praetor
prāvus, prāva, prāvum   *evil*
precēs, precum, f.pl.   *prayers*
*precor, precārī, precātus sum *pray (to)*
pretiōsus, pretiōsa, pretiōsum *expensive, precious*
*pretium, pretiī, n.   *price*
prīmō   *first, at first*
prīmum   *first*
*prīmus, prīma, prīmum   *first*
   prīmā in parte   *in the forefront*
*prīnceps, prīncipis, m.   *chief, chieftain*
*prius   *earlier*
*priusquam   *before, until*
*prō + *abl.*   *in front of, for, in return for*
probus, proba, probum   *honest*
*prōcēdō, prōcēdere, prōcessī *advance, proceed*
*procul   *far off*
prōcumbō, prōcumbere,
   prōcubuī   *fall down*
*proficīscor, proficīscī,
   profectus sum   *set out*
*prōgredior, prōgredī,
   prōgressus sum   *advance*

prohibeō, prohibēre,
   prohibuī, prohibitus   *prevent*
* prōmittō, prōmittere,
   prōmīsī, prōmissus   *promise*
prōnūntiō, prōnūntiāre,
   prōnūntiāvī, prōnūntiātus   *proclaim, preach*
* prope + *acc.*   *near*
prophēta, prophētae, m.   *prophet*
prōpōnō, prōpōnere,
   prōposuī, prōpositus   *propose, put forward*
prōsiliō, prōsilīre, prōsiluī   *leap forward, jump*
prōspectus, prōspectūs, m.   *view*
prōspiciō, prōspicere,
   prōspexī   *look out*
* proximus, proxima,
   proximum   *nearest, next to*
prūdēns, *gen.* prūdentis   *shrewd, intelligent, sensible*
psittacus, psittacī, m.   *parrot*
pūblicus, pūblica, pūblicum   *public*
* puella, puellae, f.   *girl*
* puer, puerī, m.   *boy*
* pugna, pugnae, f.   *fight*
* pugnō, pugnāre, pugnāvī   *fight*
* pulcher, pulchra, pulchrum   *beautiful*
* pulsō, pulsāre, pulsāvī,
   pulsātus   *hit, knock at, punch*
pūmiliō, pūmiliōnis, m.   *dwarf*
* pūniō, pūnīre, pūnīvī,
   pūnītus   *punish*
pūrus, pūra, pūrum   *pure, clean, spotless*
pyra, pyrae, f.   *pyre*

q

* quadrāgintā   *forty*
quaedam *see* quīdam
* quaerō, quaerere, quaesīvī,
   quaesītus   *search for, look for*
* quālis, quāle   *what sort of*
   tālis ... quālis   *such ... as*
* quam   **(1)** *how*
   quam celerrimē   *as quickly as possible*
* quam   **(2)** *than*
* quamquam   *although*
quandō   *when*
* quantus, quanta, quantum   *how big*
* quārē?   *why?*
quārtus, quārta, quārtum   *fourth*
* quasi   *as if*
* quattuor   *four*
* -que   *and*
quendam *see* quīdam
* quī, quae, quod   *who, which*
* quia   *because*
* quicquam (*also spelt*
   quidquam)   *anything*
quid? *see* quis?

* quīdam, quaedam, quoddam   *one, a certain*
quidem   *indeed*
*   nē ... quidem   *not even*
quiēs, quiētis, f.   *rest*
quiēscō, quiēscere, quiēvī   *rest*
* quīnquāgintā   *fifty*
* quīnque   *five*
quīntus, quīnta, quīntum   *fifth*
* quis? quid?   *who? what?*
quisque, quaeque, quidque   *each one*
   optimus quisque   *all the best people*
* quō?   *where? where to?*
* quō modō?   *how? in what way?*
* quod   *because*
* quondam   *one day, once*
* quoque   *also, too*
* quot?   *how many?*

r

* rapiō, rapere, rapuī, raptus   *seize, grab*
raptim   *hastily, quickly*
ratiōnēs, ratiōnum, f.pl.   *accounts*
   ratiōnēs subdūcere   *draw up accounts, write up accounts*
rē *see* rēs
rebellō, rebellāre, rebellāvī   *rebel, revolt*
rēbus *see* rēs
* recipiō, recipere, recēpī,
   receptus   *recover, take back*
   sē recipere   *recover*
recitō, recitāre, recitāvī,
   recitātus   *recite*
recumbō, recumbere, recubuī   *lie down, recline*
* recūsō, recūsāre, recūsāvī,
   recūsātus   *refuse*
* reddō, reddere, reddidī,
   redditus   *give back, make*
redēmptor, redēmptōris, m.   *contractor, builder*
* redeō, redīre, rediī   *return, go back, come back*
   redeundum est vōbīs   *you must return*
redūcō, redūcere, redūxī,
   reductus   *lead back*
* referō, referre, rettulī, relātus   *bring back, carry, deliver, tell, report*
   pedem referre   *step back*
* reficiō, reficere, refēcī,
   refectus   *repair*
* rēgīna, rēgīnae, f.   *queen*
rēgnō, rēgnāre, rēgnāvī   *reign*
* rēgnum, rēgnī, n.   *kingdom*
* regredior, regredī,
   regressus sum   *go back, return*
relēgō, relēgāre, relēgāvī,
   relēgātus   *exile*
* relinquō, relinquere, relīquī,
   relictus   *leave*

reliquus, reliqua, reliquum	*remaining*
rem *see* rēs	
remittō, remittere, remīsī,	
remissus	*send back*
rēpō, rēpere, rēpsī	*crawl*
*rēs, reī, f.	*thing*
* rē vērā	*in fact, truly, really*
rem administrāre	*manage the task*
rem cōgitāre	*consider the problem*
rem cōnficere	*finish the job*
rem nārrāre	*tell the story*
* rēs adversae	*misfortune*
*resistō, resistere, restitī	*resist*
respiciō, respicere, respexī	*look at, look upon*
*respondeō, respondēre,	
respondī	*reply*
respōnsum, respōnsī, n.	*answer*
resurgō, resurgere, resurrēxī	*rise again*
retineō, retinēre, retinuī,	
retentus	*keep, hold back*
retrō	*back*
rettulī *see* referō	
*reveniō, revenīre, revēnī	*come back, return*
revertor, revertī,	
reversus sum	*turn back, return*
revocō, revocāre, revocāvī,	
revocātus	*recall, call back*
*rēx, rēgis, m.	*king*
rhētor, rhētoris, m.	*teacher*
*rīdeō, rīdēre, rīsī	*laugh, smile*
rīpa, rīpae, f.	*river bank*
*rogō, rogāre, rogāvī, rogātus	*ask*
Rōma, Rōmae, f.	*Rome*
Rōmae	*at Rome*
Rōmānī, Rōmānōrum, m.pl.	*Romans*
Rōmānus, Rōmāna,	
Rōmānum	*Roman*
rosa, rosae, f.	*rose*
rumpō, rumpere, rūpī, ruptus	*break, split*
*ruō, ruere, ruī	*rush*
rūpēs, rūpis, f.	*rock, crag*
*rūrsus	*again*

─────────── **S** ───────────

saccārius, saccāriī, m.	*docker, dock-worker*
*sacer, sacra, sacrum	*sacred*
*sacerdōs, sacerdōtis, m.f.	*priest*
sacerdōtium, sacerdōtiī, n.	*priesthood*
sacrificium, sacrificiī, n.	*offering, sacrifice*
sacrificō, sacrificāre,	
sacrificāvī, sacrificātus	*sacrifice*
*saepe	*often*
saeviō, saevīre, saeviī	*be in a rage*
*saevus, saeva, saevum	*savage, cruel*
saltātrīx, saltātrīcis, f.	*dancing-girl*
saltō, saltāre, saltāvī	*dance*

*salūs, salūtis, f.	*safety, health*
salūtātiō, salūtātiōnis, f.	*the morning visit*
*salūtō, salūtāre, salūtāvī,	
salūtātus	*greet*
*salvē!	*hello!*
*sanguis, sanguinis, m.	*blood*
sānō, sānāre, sānāvī, sānātus	*heal, cure*
*sapiēns, *gen.* sapientis	*wise*
sarcinae, sarcinārum, f.pl.	*bags, luggage*
*satis	*enough*
*saxum, saxī, n.	*rock*
scaena, scaenae, f.	*stage, scene*
scālae, scālārum, f.pl.	*ladders*
*scelestus, scelesta, scelestum	*wicked*
*scelus, sceleris, n.	*crime*
scīlicet	*obviously*
*scindō, scindere, scidī,	
scissus	*tear, tear up*
*sciō, scīre, scīvī	*know*
*scrībō, scrībere, scrīpsī,	
scrīptus	*write*
sculpō, sculpere, sculpsī,	
sculptus	*carve*
scurrīlis, scurrīle	*rude, impudent*
*sē	*himself, herself, themselves*
inter sē	*among themselves, with*
	each other
sēcum	*with him, with her, with*
	themselves
*secō, secāre, secuī, sectus	*cut, carve*
secundus, secunda,	
secundum	*second*
secūris, secūris, f.	*axe*
secūtus *see* sequor	
*sed	*but*
*sedeō, sedēre, sēdī	*sit*
sēdēs, sēdis, f.	*seat*
sella, sellae, f.	*chair*
*semper	*always*
*senātor, senātōris, m.	*senator*
senectus, senectūtis, f.	*old age*
*senex, senis, m.	*old man*
sententia, sententiae, f.	*opinion*
*sentiō, sentīre, sēnsī, sēnsus	*feel, notice*
*septem	*seven*
*septuāgintā	*seventy*
sepulcrum, sepulcrī, n.	*tomb*
*sequor, sequī, secūtus sum	*follow*
sequēns, *gen.* sequentis	*following*
serēnus, serēna, serēnum	*calm, clear*
serviō, servīre, servīvī	*serve (as a slave)*
servitūs, servitūtis, f.	*slavery*
*servō, servāre, servāvī,	
servātus	*save, look after, preserve*
fidem servāre	*keep a promise, keep faith*
*servus, servī, m.	*slave*
sēstertius, sēstertiī, m.	*sesterce (coin)*
sēstertium vīciēns	*two million sesterces*
sevērus, sevēra, sevērum	*severe, strict*
*sex	*six*

*sexāgintā	sixty	*subitō	suddenly
*sī	if	sublātus *see* tollō	
sibi *see* sē		subscrībō, subscrībere,	
*sīc	thus, in this way	subscrīpsī, subscrīptus	sign
*sīcut	like	subterrāneus, subterrānea,	
*signum, signī, n.	sign, seal, signal	subterrāneum	underground
silentium, silentiī, n.	silence	*subveniō, subvenīre,	
sileō, silēre, siluī	be silent	subvēnī	help, come to help
*silva, silvae, f.	wood	suffīgō, suffīgere, suffīxī,	
simul	at the same time	suffīxus	nail, fasten
*simulac, simulatque	as soon as	*sum, esse, fuī	be
*sine + *abl.*	without	estō!	be!
situs, sita, situm	situated	*summus, summa, summum	highest, greatest, top
*sōl, sōlis, m.	sun	sūmptuōsus, sūmptuōsa,	
sōlācium, sōlāciī, n.	comfort	sūmptuōsum	expensive, lavish
*soleō, solēre	be accustomed	superbē	arrogantly
*sollicitus, sollicita,		*superbus, superba,	
sollicitum	worried, anxious	superbum	arrogant, proud
*sōlus, sōla, sōlum	alone, lonely, only, on one's own	*superō, superāre, superāvī,	
*sonitus, sonitūs, m.	sound	superātus	overcome, overpower
*soror, sorōris, f.	sister	superstes, superstitis, m.	survivor
sors, sortis, f.	lot	*surgō, surgere, surrēxī	get up, rise
sorte ductus	chosen by lot	suscipiō, suscipere, suscēpī,	
spargō, spargere, sparsī,		susceptus	undertake, take on
sparsus	scatter	suspīciō, suspīciōnis, f.	suspicion
*spectāculum, spectāculī, n.	show, spectacle	suspīciōsus, suspīciōsa,	
spectātor, spectātōris, m.	spectator	suspīciōsum	suspicious
*spectō, spectāre, spectāvī,		*suspicor, suspicārī,	
spectātus	look at, watch	suspicātus sum	suspect
*spernō, spernere, sprēvī,		*suus, sua, suum	his, her, their, his own, their own
sprētus	despise, reject	suī, suōrum, m.pl.	his men, his family
*spērō, spērāre, spērāvī	hope, expect		
*spēs, speī, f.	hope		
spīna, spīnae, f.	thorn, toothpick		
splendidus, splendida,			
splendidum	splendid		
sportula, sportulae, f.	handout		
stābam *see* stō			
*statim	at once		

——————— t ———————

statiō, statiōnis, f.	post	T. = Titus	
statua, statuae, f.	statue	*taberna, tabernae, f.	shop, inn
statūra, statūrae, f.	height	*taceō, tacēre, tacuī	be silent, be quiet
stēlla, stēllae, f.	star	*tacitē	quietly, silently
sternō, sternere, strāvī,		*tacitus, tacita, tacitum	quiet, silent, in silence
strātus	lay low, flatten	*tālis, tāle	such
*stō, stāre, stetī	stand	tālis ... quālis	such ... as
Stōicus, Stōicī, m.	Stoic (believer in Stoic	*tam	so
	philosophy)	*tamen	however
stola, stolae, f.	dress	tamquam	as, like
strēnuē	hard, energetically	*tandem	at last
strepitus, strepitūs, m.	noise, din	tangō, tangere, tetigī, tāctus	touch
stultitia, stultitiae, f.	stupidity	tantum	only
*stultus, stulta, stultum	stupid	*tantus, tanta, tantum	so great, such a great
*suāvis, suāve	sweet	tapēte, tapētis, n.	tapestry, wall-hanging
suāviter	sweetly	tardius	too late
*sub + *abl.*	under, beneath	taurus, taurī, m.	bull
subdūcō, subdūcere,		tē *see* tū	
subdūxī, subductus	draw up	tēctum, tēctī, n.	ceiling, roof
ratiōnēs subdūcere	draw up accounts, write up	tēgula, tēgulae, f.	tile
	accounts	temperāns, *gen.* temperantis	temperate, self-controlled
		tempestās, tempestātis, f.	storm
		*templum, templī, n.	temple

*temptō, temptāre, temptāvī, temptātus	*try*
*tempus, temporis, n.	*time*
tenebrae, tenebrārum, f.pl.	*darkness*
*teneō, tenēre, tenuī, tentus	*hold*
*terra, terrae, f.	*ground, land*
orbis terrārum	*world*
*terreō, terrēre, terruī, territus	*frighten*
terribilis, terribile	*terrible*
tertius, tertia, tertium	*third*
testāmentum, testāmentī, n.	*will*
*testis, testis, m.f.	*witness*
theātrum, theātrī, n.	*theatre*
Tiberis, Tiberis, m.	*river Tiber*
tibi *see* tū	
tībia, tībiae, f.	*pipe*
tībiīs cantāre	*play on the pipes*
tībīcen, tībīcinis, m.	*pipe player*
tignum, tignī, n.	*beam*
*timeō, timēre, timuī	*be afraid, fear*
timidē	*nervously, fearfully*
timidus, timida, timidum	*fearful, frightened*
*timor, timōris, m.	*fear*
titulus, titulī, m.	*notice, slogan, inscription, label*
toga, togae, f.	*toga*
*tollō, tollere, sustulī, sublātus	*raise, lift up, hold up*
*tot	*so many*
*tōtus, tōta, tōtum	*whole*
*trādō, trādere, trādidī, trāditus	*hand over*
*trahō, trahere, trāxī, tractus	*drag*
tranquillē	*peacefully*
*trānseō, trānsīre, trānsiī	*cross*
trānsfīgō, trānsfīgere, trānsfīxī, trānsfīxus	*pierce, stab*
trānsiliō, trānsilīre, trānsiluī	*jump through*
*trēs, tria	*three*
tribūnus, tribūnī, m.	*tribune (high-ranking officer)*
trīciēns sēstertium	*three million sesterces*
triclīnium, triclīniī, n.	*dining-room*
*trīgintā	*thirty*
*trīstis, trīste	*sad*
*tū, tuī	*you (singular)*
tuba, tubae, f.	*trumpet*
tubicen, tubicinis, m.	*trumpeter*
*tum	*then*
tum dēmum	*then at last, only then*
*turba, turbae, f.	*crowd*
*tūtus, tūta, tūtum	*safe*
*tuus, tua, tuum	*your (singular), yours*

u

*ubi	*where, when*
*ubīque	*everywhere*
ulcīscor, ulcīscī, ultus sum	*take revenge on*
*ultimus, ultima, ultimum	*furthest, last*
ultiō, ultiōnis, f.	*revenge*
umerus, umerī, m.	*shoulder*
*umquam	*ever*
ūnā cum + *abl.*	*together with*
*unda, undae, f.	*wave*
*unde	*from where*
*undique	*on all sides, from all sides*
*ūnus, ūna, ūnum	*one*
urbānus, urbāna, urbānum	*smart, fashionable*
*urbs, urbis, f.	*city*
usquam	*anywhere*
usque ad + *acc.*	*right up to*
*ut	*(1) as*
*ut	*(2) that, so that, in order that*
*utrum	*whether*
utrum ... an	*whether ... or*
utrum ... necne	*whether ... or not*
*uxor, uxōris, f.	*wife*

v

vacuus, vacua, vacuum	*empty*
*valdē	*very much, very*
*valē	*goodbye, farewell*
valēdīcō, valēdīcere, valēdīxī	*say goodbye*
valētūdō, valētūdinis, f.	*health*
*vehementer	*violently, loudly*
*vehō, vehere, vexī, vectus	*carry*
*vel	*or*
velim, vellem *see* volō	
vēnālīcius, vēnālīciī, m.	*slave-dealer*
*vēndō, vēndere, vēndidī, vēnditus	*sell*
*venēnum, venēnī, n.	*poison*
venia, veniae, f.	*mercy*
*veniō, venīre, vēnī	*come*
venter, ventris, m.	*stomach*
*ventus, ventī, m.	*wind*
Venus, Veneris, f.	*Venus (goddess of love)*
verber, verberis, n.	*blow*
*verberō, verberāre, verberāvī, verberātus	*strike, beat*
*verbum, verbī, n.	*word*
versus, versūs, m.	*verse, line of poetry*
*vertō, vertere, vertī, versus	*turn*
vertor, vertī, versus sum	*turn*
*vērum, vērī, n.	*truth, the truth*
*vērus, vēra, vērum	*true, real*
* rē vērā	*in fact, truly, really*
*vester, vestra, vestrum	*your (plural)*
*vestīmenta, vestīmentōrum, n.pl.	*clothes*
vestrum *see* vōs	
vetus, *gen.* veteris	*old*
*vexō, vexāre, vexāvī, vexātus	*annoy*

vī *see* vīs

*via, viae, f. — *street, way*

    Via Sacra, Viae Sacrae, f. — *the Sacred Way (road running through the Forum)*

vīciēns sēstertium — *two million sesterces*

victima, victimae, f. — *victim*

victor, victōris, m. — *victor, winner*

victōria, victōriae, f. — *victory*

victus *see* vincō

*videō, vidēre, vīdī, vīsus — *see*

videor, vidērī, vīsus sum — *seem*

vigilō, vigilāre, vigilāvī — *stay awake*

*vīgintī — *twenty*

vīlla, vīllae, f. — *house, villa*

*vinciō, vincīre, vīnxī, vīnctus — *bind, tie up*

*vincō, vincere, vīcī, victus — *conquer, win, be victorious*

*vīnum, vīnī, n. — *wine*

*vir, virī, m. — *man*

vīrēs, vīrium, f.pl — *strength*

virgō, virginis, f. — *virgin*

*virtūs, virtūtis, f. — *courage*

vīs, f. — *force, violence*

vīsitō, vīsitāre, vīsitāvī, vīsitātus — *visit*

vīsus *see* videō

*vīta, vītae, f. — *life*

    vītam agere — *lead a life*

vitium, vitiī, n. — *sin*

*vītō, vītāre, vītāvī, vītātus — *avoid*

*vituperō, vituperāre, vituperāvī, vituperātus — *blame, curse*

*vīvō, vīvere, vīxī — *live, be alive*

*vīvus, vīva, vīvum — *alive, living*

*vix — *hardly, scarcely, with difficulty*

vōbīs *see* vōs

vōcem *see* vōx

*vocō, vocāre, vocāvī, vocātus — *call*

*volō, velle, voluī — *want*

    velim — *I should like*

*volvō, volvere, volvī, volūtus — *turn, roll*

    in animō volvere — *wonder, turn over in the mind*

*vōs — *you (plural)*

    vōbīscum — *with you (plural)*

*vōx, vōcis, f. — *voice*

*vulnerō, vulnerāre, vulnerāvī, vulnerātus — *wound, injure*

*vulnus, vulneris, n. — *wound*

*vultus, vultūs, m. — *expression, face*